T0338315

# Living Rooms as FACTORIES

*Class, Gender, and the Satellite Factory System in Taiwan*

# Living Rooms as
# FACTORIES

*Class, Gender, and the
Satellite Factory System in Taiwan*

**Ping-Chun Hsiung**

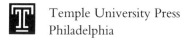

Temple University Press
Philadelphia

Temple University Press, Philadelphia 19122
Copyright © 1996 by Ping-Chun Hsiung
All rights reserved
Published 1996
Printed in the United States of America

&infin; The paper used in this publication meets the requirements of the
American National Standard for Information Sciences—Permanence of
Paper for Printed Library Materials, ANSI Z39.48-1984

Text design by Eliz. Anne O'Donnell


Library of Congress Cataloging-in-Publication Data
Hsiung, Ping-Chun, 1954–
    Living rooms as factories : class, gender, and the satellite factory
system in Taiwan = [K'o t'ing chi kung ch'ang] / Ping-Chun
Hsiung.
        p.   cm.
    Parallel title in Chinese characters.
    Includes bibliographical references and index.
    ISBN 1-56639-389-2 (cloth : alk. paper). — ISBN 1-56639-390-6
(paper : alk. paper)
    1. Home labor—Taiwan.   2. Women—Employment—Taiwan.
3. Working class—Taiwan.   I. Title
HD2336.T28H75   1996
331.4'25—dc20                                                    95-42430

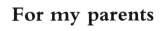
For my parents

# Contents

# Acknowledgments

This is a personal journey based on collective support. My intellectual debts go to my teachers at UCLA: Drs. Lucie Cheng, Ruth Milkman, Francesca Bray, and Karen B. Sacks. As the manuscript was reviewed, I received critical and generous feedback from a number of reviewers. Even though I have not incorporated all their responses, their comments and questions helped me to clarify my thinking and strengthen my arguments. Joan Campbell's editorial assistance and insights have improved the presentation of this book tremendously.

I thank my parents who value education more than anything else. Defying a precarious financial situation, and at great personal sacrifice, they put five of us through higher education. I am indebted to my father who treasures his daughters as much as his sons, and to my mother who believes there is no way that her daughters are inferior to anyone's sons. This is a work in memory of my mother-in-law, Hui-Ying J. Ho. My relationship with her helped me to understand better how Chinese women deal with the suffering, pain, and powerlessness inflicted on them by their society.

This research would have been impossible if I had not received help from all the owners and workers I met in the factories. I appreciated the chance to work with them. As to the married women, I thank them for sharing their lives with me. I learned a great deal from the way they handle hardships and manage to enjoy life.

Support and friendship from Raymond Sirgist, Michael Hui, and most recently Cynthia McLean have been extremely valuable to my own thinking and practices of Taoism and *Wuwei* amid some most trying times. They are the treasure of my life. Special thanks go to my husband, Yu-Nan Ho, whose relaxed style and sense of humor have made it possible for his partner to complete a dream of her own.

Acknowledgment is given to the following sources for permission to use material from their publications:  Tables 1.11 through 1.14 are compiled from data from Bier Chou, "Industrialization and change in women's status: A reevaluation of some data from Taiwan," in *Taiwan: A newly industrialized state*, ed. Hsin-huang Michael Hsiao, Wei-yuan Cheng, and Hou-sheng Chan (Taipei: Department of Sociology, National Taiwan University, 1989). An earlier version of the introduction on my fieldwork appears in "Between bosses and workers: The dilemma of a keen observer and a vocal feminist," in *Feminist dilemmas in fieldwork*, ed. Diana L. Wolf (Boulder, Colo.: Westview Press, forthcoming).

All Chinese names and words are romanized in pinyin unless they come from Chinese sources, where the Wade-Giles system has been used.

This research has received financial support from the Center of Pacific Rim Studies at UCLA, the Women's Research Program at National Taiwan University, and Chiang Ching-Kuo Foundation for International Scholarly Exchange. The Pacific Cultural Foundation in the Republic of China has provided a publication grant.

# Introduction

This study is about the employment experiences and the family lives of married women in Taiwan's satellite factory system. It analyzes how Taiwan's "economic miracle" comes about in a local and daily way through the work and family lives of married women. From the theoretical perspective, it explores the intersections between capitalist logic and patriarchal practices, the interplay of class formation and gender stratification, and the linkage between the individual, family/factory, state, and global restructuring. The book's title, *Living Rooms as Factories (Keting Ji Kongchang)*, is taken from a slogan employed by the Taiwanese government in its developmental programs that promote homework and thereby foster married women's labor force participation. I use it to highlight the particularity of Taiwan's economic development, the special roles played in it by the state, and married women's significant contribution to it.

The satellite factory system is a concept constructed to study a hierarchical subcontracting manufacturing system that consists of numerous small-scale, family-centered, and export-oriented factories. Most of these factories are located in urban residential neighborhoods, at the fringes of urban-rural conjunctions, or in peasants' front yards that were formerly used to dry grain. Inside the factory, youngsters run around while their mothers are busy polishing, assembling, packing, and packaging. Often these women are planning what to make for dinner; many have their babies on their backs. These factories usually further contract work out to homeworkers whose living rooms are converted for factory production.

The word *satellite* is translated literally from the Chinese words 衛星 *(weixing)*. The Chinese emphasizes the interconnections among

1

these factories and their links with international markets. As part of a production system, a chain of several factories is involved to manufacture a single product, with individual factories producing parts only. By small-scale, I mean factories with fewer than thirty workers. The size is chosen on two grounds. First, under Taiwan's current Standard Labor Law, unionization is not allowed in factories with fewer than thirty workers. This prohibition is essential to my analysis of labor control on the shop floor and labor politics in the workplace. Second, even though the number thirty is not an exact cut off point, factories with a significantly greater number of employees are organized very differently, as far as production, management, and workforce composition are concerned.

Over the last three decades, Taiwan's widely recognized "economic miracle" has produced an average 9.1 percent annual growth in gross national product, as against an average of 6.9 percent for the United States (Wu and Chow 1992). Much of Taiwan's economic progress has been made by its export sector: in the early 1950s, only 8.6 percent of the gross national product (GNP) was contributed by exports; but by the mid-1970s, the export sector accounted for fully 54.3 percent of Taiwan's GNP. Even under the impact of protectionism in the 1980s, the export sector still contributed 41.4 percent of Taiwan's GNP (Wu and Chow 1992, 8–9). By 1990, Taiwan had become the thirteenth-largest trading nation in the world, with a US$88 billion trove of foreign reserves (Time, 1992, September 7). The GNP per capita increased from US$154 in 1960 to US$7,332 in 1990, bringing Taiwan out of the so-called underdeveloped category.

Taiwan's economic growth ran parallel to the restructuring of the international market. The market, once dominated by the mass production of the First World, has gradually been seized by the newly established factories of Third World countries.[1] In 1965 the United States had a trade surplus of approximately US$1.9 billion with the developing countries. By 1988 this had been converted into a trade deficit of more than US$45 billion dollars. The reliance of the First World upon the Third World for manufactured goods, and the structural shift from exporter/supplier to importer/buyer has been categorized as global restructuring (Ward, 1990). In this restructuring, the so-called Four Dragons—that is, South Korea, Taiwan, Hong Kong, and Singapore—have played vital roles. In 1965 less than 7 percent of U.S. imports from the developing countries came from the Four Dragons. By 1988 these four countries supplied about 41 percent of U.S. imports from the same

TABLE I.1

Sources of Imports to the United States, Selected Years
(billion U.S. dollars)

|  | 1965 | 1970 | 1975 | 1980 | 1985 | 1988 |
|---|---|---|---|---|---|---|
| Taiwan | 93 | 549 | 1,946 | 6,854 | 16,396 | 24,804 |
| Hong Kong | 343 | 944 | 1,573 | 4,739 | 8,396 | 10,243 |
| South Korea | 54 | 370 | 1,442 | 4,147 | 10,013 | 20,189 |
| Singapore | — | 81 | 553 | 1,921 | 4,260 | 7,996 |
| Total | 490 | 1,944 | 5,514 | 24,515 | 39,065 | 63,232 |
| Third World | 7,145 | 10,442 | 39,311 | 117,025 | 116,161 | 153,127 |

SOURCE: *Statistical Abstract of the United States,* various years.

category (see Table I.1). Among the Four Dragons, Taiwan has become the largest supplier, accounting for 16 percent of American imports from the Third World in 1988, and enjoyed a trade surplus of $13.9 billion in 1989.

Many developing countries, in the process of industrialization, have experienced an influx of foreign capital, the establishment of large multinational corporations in export processing zones sponsored by the state, and the inflow of young single girls to work in the new factories. What sets Taiwan apart from most of the others is a remarkable reliance upon numerous small-scale, family-centered, and export-oriented subcontracting factories outside the export processing zones.[2] In fact, over the last two decades, about 85 percent of the factories in Taiwan's manufacturing sector had fewer than thirty workers. Hence, it is not too much to claim that Taiwan's satellite factories have been at the core of the country's "economic miracle."

However, our current understanding of Taiwan's export-led economy and its effects on women have mainly derived from the literature concerning women's labor force participation. Studies analyzing statistical data identify either the recent increases in female labor force participation (Liu 1984; Y. Liu 1985; Chiang and Ku 1985; Tsay 1985, Liu and Hwang 1987), the overall difference in patterns of labor force participation between men and women (Greenhalgh 1985; B. Chou 1989), or factors contributing to that difference. Other case studies complement the quantitative figures by bringing women's voices into the picture. In order to find out how paid employment affects women, researchers have focused on the work experiences and family status of young single women who were recruited by newly established large factories in the 1970s (Arrigo 1980, 1984; Diamond 1979; Kung 1976, 1983, 1984). They were mainly interested in discovering under what conditions these young women are hired, how much money they send back to their families, and how much say they have in whom they marry.

The focus of these studies on young single women in the large newly established factories may be due to the fact that they were conducted in the 1970s when the influx of young single women was at its height.[3] As a result, we know very little about workers in the majority of Taiwain's factories, that is, those with fewer than thirty workers. Nor do we know what happened to the first cohort of Taiwanese factory daughters when they married. My effort to fill this void first started in the last years of my graduate studies when I became interested in the work, marriage, and family experiences of Taiwan's first cohort of factory girls.

At the beginning, I encountered two different pictures. On the one hand, some studies document that most of the factory girls were forced to resign when they married (Kung 1983; Lu 1984). This conclusion is confirmed by Hill Gates' pioneering work on class formation in Taiwan's economic development process. Gates uses the term "part-time proletarians" to emphasize that workers in Taiwan only spend a few years of their lives working in the factory. Once married, both men and women look for opportunities outside the factory system (Gates, 1979). On the other hand, a few reports did record the existence of a large number of married women in the small factories (Niehoff 1987; Stites 1982, 1985). Their observations were supported by what I had witnessed as a junior school teacher in a fishing village in the central part of Taiwan in the mid-1970s. On regular visits to my students' families, I saw that toys, plastic flowers, and Christmas ornaments were made by my female students, their aunts, and their mothers. "These are for the Americans," I was told. My hunch then was that, after they were married, Taiwan's first cohort of factory girls might have moved from the large factories to small ones in their neighborhoods or worked as homeworkers for these satellite factories on a piece-rate basis.

My intellectual interest in resolving the contradictory reports intersected with my personal trajectory as a Chinese feminist. As an indigenous Chinese researcher, I have many advantages. Knowing the language, ecological environment, and cultural norms and practices in

Taiwan put me on a par with my Chinese colleagues. At the same time, as a researcher influenced by Western feminist scholarship, I viewed existing class and gender inequalities in Taiwan with a critical eye.[4]

Because I wanted to take a fresh look at what was going on in the factories, participant observation seemed to be the best approach. Before I began my fieldwork, I was warned that tensions between management and workers might create difficulties for me if I intended to cover both sides of the story. People suggested that I avoid possible disaster by studying the position of either the management or the workers. I decided to focus on the workers, if I had to choose between the two.

In the summer of 1989, I spent three months in satellite factories that made wooden jewelry boxes, working in six and visiting about thirty others. Most of them were located in the central part of Taiwan. In December 1989 and January 1990, I revisited the factories and talked to the people I had met on my first trip.

In the field, I was seen, treated, and approached simultaneously as an insider and an outsider. From the standpoint of people in the factory, my outsider status came from what I did (studying in the States), while my insider status came from who I was (an indigenous woman). Our shared experiences made it easy to get on a friendly footing in the factory. For example, during a break, an owner's mother, a widow in her midseventies, told me what types of odd jobs she had done to raise her children. When she described how hard it was to make straw hats at night under oil lights, I understood what she said because my family once lived in a remote mountain village where there was no electricity or running water. As a child, I did my homework by candlelight, and my sister and I used to carry water from a mountain spring an hour away from our home. On another occasion, I talked with several male factory owners about the games we used to play in the rice fields when there were no video games, no Ninja Turtles, and no high-rise buildings.

My coworkers' curiosity about my life and experiences in the United States allowed them to relate to me as both insider and outsider. The fact that I had to make extra efforts to get rice from Chinese grocery stores in Monterey Park, California, brought comments such as "We never realized it could be an issue" and "I could never live without rice." My coworkers were surprised but delighted to learn that, rather than beef steak, my favorite dish was bitter melon, a vegetable that is very popular in Taiwan but only available in a few Chinese grocery stores in the United States. I told a coworker in her early sixties that I once dreamed of a bitter melon dish, "but because I was too excited, I woke up before I had a chance to taste it in my dream." The few times I was invited to her home after that, she made sure that there was bitter melon on the table. When she and I went to their garden patch in the middle of the rice field, to pick some herbs and dig out some sweet potatoes for a special soup I had not had since my family left that mountain village, I felt as if I had come home at last.

To me, working in the factory was like experiencing a life I had just luckily escaped by a small margin. Throughout the years, it has been clear to me that my continuing advancement in higher education owed less to my school performance and more to my father, who treasures his daughters as much as his sons, and to my mother, who believes that there is no way that her daughters are inferior to anyone's sons. By the time I got into university, many of my girlfriends from elementary school were married. As I move on to various stages of my life, I have never stopped wondering what would have happened if the girl sitting next to me in fifth grade had been given the same opportunity her brothers or I had, and what has happened to the female students I taught in the fishing village. When my coworkers told me stories about their work experiences and family lives, I felt as though my childhood girlfriends or my former students were telling me what had happened to them since I left.

Once in the field, despite the warnings I had been given, it soon became clear to me that covering both sides of the story was the only way to go. Because factories ranged in size from three to thirty workers, it was virtually impossible to get access to workers without the consent of their bosses. Not only was interacting with the bosses essential for my data-collection purposes; listening to them talking about their operating strategies also helped me to understand the structural constraints experienced by Third world exporters. Focusing exclusively on factory workers not only proved to be technically problematic, but would also have left me with an incomplete picture.

My entry to the factories was granted by the owners partly because of the identity they perceived us to share. I was welcomed as someone who recognized the contribution that the small-scale factories have made to Taiwan's export-led economy, as well as the hardships that they have endured along the way. My presence was further appreciated by the owners because I worked for free. One owner even tried to prolong my stay when I was preparing to move on to another factory. Another claimed, "If we were to pay you, you would feel obligated to work like a real worker" (meaning to keep up with the same productivity level). The calculating manner in which the owners dealt with my labor was a source of tension throughout my fieldwork. In the last week of my stay, I learned indirectly that the reason one of the factory owners had acted aloof was that I was not willing to work in his factory for more than two weeks. According to my source of information, the owner would not talk to me in depth unless I agreed to work there for at least a month.

Because the factories were small, it did not take long for me to know every worker on the shop floor. I was quickly accepted as an insider by the workers and was frequently laughed at as being incapable of working as hard as they. My relationships with female coworkers were especially rewarding. One old lady in a factory started to tell others in the village that I was her daughter. Concerned about my future, she questioned whether I would ever be able to get a job simply by knowing how to read books. Before I left, she told me to call on her if I ever had trouble finding a job. She said, "We can always get you something here in the factory. Don't worry." Another female worker in her early sixties, who was still involved in matchmaking, taught me all the tricks one needed to become a popular and successful matchmaker, so that I would be able to surmount any future financial hardships. "I am sure even in America there are people who want to get married but don't know who is available. If you talk to people regularly, matchmaking is really easy," she said.

Along with this friendship and acceptance came the pressures that I felt after my coworkers learned about my personal background. They were very surprised that I did not have a child although I had been married for many years. Their instinctive response was "Have you seen a doctor?" On one occasion, a group of female homeworkers told me unanimously that I should have at least one son to perpetuate my husband's family name, since he is his parents' only son. On another occasion, a woman offered to tell me how to ensure that I get a son in my first pregnancy. The fact that I stayed in my parents' house, rather than with my in-laws, as also an issue of general concern. One female worker asked me whether I had gone back to my husband's family or my own family when I had first arrived in Taiwan. I learned later that her in-laws had granted her only two visits to her parents in the fourteen years of her marriage.

My efforts to cover the perspectives of both factory bosses and workers ran up against my political concern for the workers' welfare. In order to capture and understand how workers in general, and female workers in particular, are perceived by their bosses, I had to subdue the feminist and political beliefs that had brought me there in the first place. Thus, instead of jumping to a quick conclusion, I calmly asked a male factory owner to explain why he believed that female homeworkers were "petty minded." As an indigenous feminist researcher, I was inspired by and drawn to my female coworkers' inner strength and their gutsy and determined personalities. My feminism and compassion put me in touch with the pain and triumph of my coworkers; but I had to hold back my impatient reaction to those who weren't taking any action. After carefully documenting women's actions and inactions, I came to see that battles that have never been fought tell as much about the system as battles that have been won. As I witnessed the government's power over workers in general, and working-class women in particular, I was led to explore the state policy on labor control and its "Living Rooms as Factories" program.

In the field I juggled two modes of self-presentation every day: a keen observer on the one hand and a vocal feminist on the other. Looking back, I realize that I was in constant negotiation with the very system, and the agents of that system—most of them men—that I had set out to study. This negotiation process gave me firsthand experience of patriarchal and capitalist control in Taiwan's satellite factory system. These personal experiences provided invaluable insights and eventually helped me to tease out both subtle and the not so subtle mechanisms that underlie class and gender relations in Taiwan's satellite factory system.

In the end, I came to question the dichotomous conceptualization of the power relationship between female ethnographers and female informants presented in recent discussions of feminist methodology (Patai 1991; Stacy 1991; Acker et al. 1991). These focus on the intrusion and intervention of the researcher into the lives of female informants, the appropriation of the informants' private emotions and stories by the researcher, and the dominant position of the researcher in presentation and representation of the researched. I challenge this model by pointing out the multidimensional power relationships, of which the patriarchal/capitalist system, individual agents of the system, female informants, and female feminist researchers are the key constituents. I argue that a multidimensional portrayal of power relationships provides a contextual framework in which the feminist researcher can best explore how power structures are constructed and contested through everyday interaction between the dominator and the dominated (Hsiung, forthcoming).

Generally speaking, the ethnographic data on the organization of the satellite factory system, on its labor process, and on workers' resistance, come mainly from my first trip, when I worked in the factories. During my second trip I gathered information about how the factory, its workers, and the workers' families cope with the seasonal fluctuation of production. My interaction with workers in the factories was more relaxed during the second trip because winter is the slack season. However, my initial plan to conduct in-depth interviews with the married female workers whom I had met during the preceding summer proved unworkable because, upon arriving at the women's homes, I was often greeted by the women's husbands. Conversation was dominated by their husbands even though many of the female workers had proved very articulate when I talked with them in the workplace. As a result, when I sat down to analyze the ethnographic data, I realized that I could not talk about women's work and family lives without discussing their relationship with husbands and male coworkers. Nor is it possible to understand workers' employment experiences without taking their interaction with their employers into account. Therefore, although the book's main focus is on the family and working experiences of married women, I will also be referring throughout to men and employers to illustrate the interplay of gender and class in the satellite factory system.

In my analysis I treat patriarchy and capitalism as interlocking systems. Patriarchy mainly takes the form of institutional forces that define and sustain male domination and female subordination in household production. Capitalism here denotes means and mechanisms that ensure surplus labor appropriation in the satellite factory system.[5] Together, they form the material foundation and ideological parameters within which married female workers endure their everyday trials and achieve their triumphs.

My discussion of class and gender relations, although focused on Taiwan, has broader relevance and raises a number of interesting theoretical issues. For instance, the decline of the agricultural economy in the course of economic development, a prominent feature of the Taiwanese experience, has brought about similar changes in social structure and everyday life in many Third World countries. As the agricultural sector shrinks, peasant families begin to engage in commercial farming or migrate to urban centers for newly available jobs in the manufacturing sector. In Taiwan small-scale manufacturing production was pursued by families as their survival strategy. Fathers often converted land and family treasure into capital, in order to set up small factories. In this way, they hoped to attract their sons back from the cities and keep the extended family together. "Machines, instead of land, became the new means of production and thus contributed to the cementing of father-son relations" (Hu 1984, 119). As small-scale factory production gradually extended into local communities, apartment dwellers in the inner city began to complain about the noise from the upstairs neighbors who had recently converted their living rooms into underground factories (Hsu, 1976). The family-centered aspects of these small-scale factories were not entirely new to working-class people in Taiwan. Small food stands on the street corner, barbershops in the village, or convenience stores in the neighborhood are normally run by a couple with help from their children (Gates, 1987). What is new, however, is that these small local factories form a socioeconomic system that generates and mobilizes local resources to serve international demand. Studying the dynamic of macro and micro forces in Taiwan during its transformation from an agricultural into an export-oriented manufacturing economy can thus shed light on the phenomenon of economic development more generally. Similarly, by analyzing the interrelationship between women and the state in a particular developing economy, my book makes a contribution to the broader topic of women and development.

Inspired by feminist research on women's productive and reproductive labor, this study also looks at the gender division of labor within the family and factory. Married women in Taiwan's satellite factory system are not alone as they seek to carve out a niche at the intersections of capitalist logic and patriarchal practices. The lace makers in Narsapur, India, skillfully carry out both their productive and reproductive responsibilities. As housewives, they spend most of their morning hours on household chores. As workers producing for the world market, they put in an additional six to eight hours every day doing homework (Mies 1982). It has also been well documented that married women caring for young children either withdraw from formal employment temporarily or engage in part-time, informal work through subcontracting. Therefore, as one looks into women's work experiences, it becomes clear that the issue is not so much whether or not they have ever been integrated into the labor market. Rather, one needs to ask how these women reconcile their "work" with their domestic duties. Thus, although I rely on narratives of Taiwanese women to unravel the intertwined productive and reproductive labor of women, my findings have implications for women elsewhere.

The oppressive conditions found in Taiwan's satellite factory system—low wages, poor working environment, severe labor control—are common to many developing countries. Even in the United States, with its highly developed economy, numerous sweatshops continue to operate under similar conditions (Beneria and Roldan 1987; Sassen-Koob 1989; Stepick 1989; Fernandez-Kelly and Garcia 1989). The garment industry in large cities such as Miami, Los Angeles, and New York is notorious for taking advantage of female illegal workers and recent immigrants. Scholars therefore no longer conceptualize the unregulated and decentralized economic activities in the informal sector as transitory phenomena confined to the Third World (Portes, Castells, and Benton 1989; Beneria and Roldan 1987; Portes and Sassen-Koob 1987). Instead, these conditions are viewed as the by-products of capital accumulation on a global scale. For example, Mies (1988) showed that, after the Third World was integrated into the global economy, women were pushed into low-wage or nonwage labor, while Bennholdt-Thomsen (1988) demonstrated the importance of unwaged labor to the global economy. According to Bennholdt-Thomsen, surplus value from wage labor constitutes only a very small segment of capital accumulation globally. As capitalism advances, workers are incorporated into the system as unwaged laborers through a process of "housewifization." Similarly, Werlhof (1988) maintained that proletarian labor is increasingly replaced by labor that "bears the characteristics of housework, . . . labor not protected by trade unions or labor laws, that is available at any time, for any price." These new trends of deregulation, informalization, and feminization have enabled an increasing number of factories to reduce their reliance on permanent full-time wage workers as more and more casual and piece-rate workers are hired through subcontracting (Standing, 1989). Thus the everyday struggles between bosses and workers in Taiwanese factories I visited undoubtedly resemble what goes on in workplaces around the world, wherever informal and unregulated labor is the norm.

Against this general background, I intend to address three specific questions: first, how an "economic miracle" based on the principle of "living rooms as factories" comes about at the local and everyday level; second, how these factories survive and stay competitive in the global context; and third, what it means to men and women to be incorporated into a productive system that is small in scale, family centered, and export oriented.

## Women and Development in Taiwan

My initial curiosity about the lives of the first cohort of Taiwan's factory daughters after they are married took me to small factories in rice fields, sweatshops on the back streets and alleys, and families' living rooms. There, I found that a significant number of this first cohort of factory daughters continued to work in the manufacturing sector after marriage. Until recently, however, this phenomenon has received very little scholarly attention. For many older women, moreover, working for these factories was their first nonagricultural employment. As the project unfolded, I became increasingly convinced that it is essential to include married women's experiences in the satellite factory system as part of any research directed toward women and economic development in Taiwan. Most factories in Taiwan's export sector are very small, and since the 1970s the rate of increase in married women's labor-force participation has been higher than that of single women. Our understanding of women and development in Taiwan is therefore incomplete without careful analysis of married women's experiences in the satellite factory system.

When I looked closely at changes in women's everyday lives brought about by Taiwan's industrialization, I was struck by the fact that patriarchal norms and practices tended to emerge in a new guise. One such change was reported in 1984 by Tai-Li Hu, an anthropologist who thought nothing would surprise her anymore after staying in New York City for several years. Hu was shocked by what she saw in her mother-in-law's village in central Taiwan. It took her a while to figure out how it could be that "a boy of nineteen slept with his girlfriend at his home, and his parents did not say a word" (Hu 1984, 121). Apparently premarital chastity, once highly valued in Chinese society, becomes relatively less important when the groom's family can get a better bride price if a pregnant bride is involved. Having the wedding on a specific "good day" chosen by a geomancer is negotiable, if by delaying the marriage the bride's family can get several more months of their daughter's wages (Hu, 1984). Likewise, what women in the field told me about their first years of marriage gave a very different picture from that described in Margery

Wolf's work on women and family in rural Taiwan during the late 1950s and early 1960s.

In an agricultural economy, the primary responsibility of a daughter-in-law was to bear a new generation, especially sons, for her husband's family. This is probably why women's procreative capacity plays such a critical role in Wolf's analytical framework of the uterine family. According to Wolf, Taiwanese women could only manipulate the patrilineal, patrilocal, and patriarchal family system by creating their own uterine families, in which their sons, and daughters to a lesser extent, are the immediate members. A woman's intimate ties with members of her uterine family ensured her financial and emotional security in an otherwise hostile familial environment. Perhaps for this reason, married women's roles in the *productive* sphere appeared to be less important, if not nonexistent, in Wolf's study of rural women in Taiwan (M. Wolf, 1972).[6]

As industrialization proceeded, even though women continued to be molded into dutiful wives, mothers, and daughters-in-law at marriage, they were now simultaneously transformed into productive laborers (paid or unpaid) by and in Taiwan's satellite factory system. Women are now expected to produce another generation of laborers while acting as workers themselves. The narratives I heard about women's first years of marriage illustrate the continued viability of patriarchal norms during very rapid industrial transformation. The expectations men have about their wives suggest that the satellite factory system represents the latest version of the Chinese family—a locus where capitalist logic and patriarchal practices intersect.

My call for an amended notion of the "uterine family" finds an echo with Ellen Oxfeld's recent work on family enterprise among the ethnic Chinese in Calcutta, India (Oxfeld, 1993). Oxfeld argues that married women employ means other than close emotional bonds to cement the "uterine family" and thereby enhance their well-being in the family. In an urban entrepreneurial context, married women's productive labor serves multiple purposes. According to Oxfeld, family members and local communities praise married women who are active and diligent in the family business. Such a reputation is essential as it ensures a married woman's status in her husband's family. Besides, the sacrifices of a hardworking mother are often essential to secure her son's loyalty and support. In other words, in the nonagricultural economy, close emotional bonds with their sons are no longer sufficient to guarantee the financial well-being of married women.

Married women's new roles in the productive and reproductive spheres also led me to explore several theoretical issues that have not been studied previously. The fist set of these issues concerns how women of different social classes interact and to what extent their experiences overlap and diverge. The existing literature on women in Taiwan focuses either on working-class women (Arrigo 1980, 1984; Kung 1976; R. Gallin 1984a, 1984b) or the professional and middle classes (Diamond 1973a, 1973b, 1975; T.-K. Hsu 1989, 1992; Yao 1981; *Zhongguo Luntan* 1989). The satellite factory system turns out to be an ideal arena to study tensions among women across class lines, as some women achieve higher status as the owner's wives while others remain simply homeworkers and wage workers. Based on women's position in relation to the productive system, I examine the conditions under which women of different groups are pitted against one another. I also show where and how women's experiences overlap regardless of their differing social positions. From the theoretical perspective, the experiences of the owners' wives allow me to disentangle the tension between women's class and gender identities.

## Women, the State, and Taiwan's Economic Development

Throughout the years, economists and political scientists interested in Taiwan's economic accomplishments have paid much attention to the contributing factors at the macro level (Myers 1986; Lau 1990; Ranis 1979; Fei et al 1979). In the area of state and economic development, for example, the main emphasis has been on the state's strategic guidance and intervention roles in finance, infrastructure, and the domestic market (Deyo 1987; Henderson and Appelbaum 1992; Gereffi 1989; Castells 1992). This approach, although valuable, fails to examine the implications of state policies at the micro level. Nor does it take into account the sacrifices and contributions of individual men and women as they carry out these policies.

To remedy these failings, I employ statistical as well as ethnographic data to analyze the relationship of macro and micro forces in a period of dramatic socioeconomic change. In order to disentangle the relationship among gender, state, and Taiwan's economic development, I examine the implications of state policies for class formation and gender stratification. My analysis has its origin in existing studies of the relation-ship between women and the state.

Based on empirical data, scholars have argued that the National-ist Party (the Kuomintang, hereafter KMT) has actively fostered women's subordination. Women's status in Taiwan is not simply a con-tinuation of traditional values and culture. Instead, it is a product of pa-triarchal capitalism, by which the interests of the capitalist, the state, and the international market are served (Gates 1979). Because of the KMT's conservative position, younger women of the middle class who grew up under the KMT regime were less likely to hold paid employment after marriage than women of the older generation who developed their iden-tity in the 1930s when liberalism was prominent (Diamond 1973a, 1973b, 1975).[7] Since the state allocates a large share of its budget to mil-itary expenses, it has failed to provide adequate welfare services for work-ing-class families. This lack of services has meant that unless younger women can find child care support, they cannot take advantage of new opportunities to achieve autonomy through labor-force participation. For their part, older women often shoulder household chores and child-care responsibilities in exchange for the daily care needed in their old age (R. Gallin 1984a, 1985b).

This body of literature, along with my fieldwork observations, in-spired me to go further and examine the dilemmas posed by the need to reconcile the potential conflict between the capitalists' interest in having plenty of cheap labor and the patriarchal demand for the unconditional ser-vice of full-time housewives in the home. I will address this topic in Chap-ter 2 where I analyze the "Living Rooms as Factories" program and the "Mothers Workshops," two major campaigns of the KMT's Community Development Program that attempted to incorporate married women into productive labor while instructing them to remain morally obligated to contribute to Taiwan's economic development through fulfillment of their traditional duties in the family as wives, mothers, and caretakers.

At the theoretical level, my inquiry echoes Hill Gates' effort to understand the origin of Chinese capitalism in the Sung dynasty (960–1279 A.D.) (Gates 1989). In her analysis Gates proposes two distinguish-able but interacting modes of production. The tributary mode of pro-duction (hereafter, TMP) functioned to generate revenues from the commoners for the state, which consisted of the emperor and his func-tionaires. The petty capitalist mode of production (hereafter PCMP) op-erated to extract surplus values from propertyless households for the benefit of households that owned private means of production. According to Gates, the relationship between TMP and PCMP was paradoxical. On the one hand, the TMP and PCMP stood in conflict because unlimited expansion of the latter could become a fertile ground for powerful clans that could challenge the official state. On the other hand, the TMP and PCMP were interrelated because both drew on neo-Confucianism to define and maintain a hierarchal sociopolitical order. The hierarchal order was critical because it enabled the emperor to extract labor, taxes, and services from his subjects. For the PCMP, neo-Confucianism not only taught the propertyless to accept their subordination, but its doctrine on gender relations also legitimized women's subordination, and hence capital accumulation, through the appropriation of women's productive and reproductive labor.

Although Gates' work deals with the emergence of capitalism in premodern China, it is pertinent to our understanding of Taiwan's economic development in the 20th century. First of all, it is fruitful to articulate the state and the petty capitalist as operating in separate but interrelated domains. In contemporary Taiwan, the tension between the state and independent petty capitalists appears to be less prominent than it was in premodern China. By the time the KMT state launched the export-oriented economic program, it had virtually no potential rival on the island.[8] Besides, as rightly pointed out by a number of scholars, the KMT state has a stake in the expansion of small manufacturing production because its political legitimacy is based upon Taiwan's economic prosperity (Amsden 1979; Gates 1981; Myers 1986). Thus relations between the state and the petty capitalist class are fairly close. Indeed, the KMT has adopted a number of procapitalist strategies to ensure a thriving petty capitalist class. My analysis of the nature of procapitalist strategies adopted by the KMT state takes into account the historic specifics of Taiwan's economic development.

Second, in premodern China, although women's subordinate position was essential to capital accumulation by the petty capitalists, gender stratification served no direct function in the TMP. The development of capitalism in contemporary Taiwan tells a different story. The state's political fate is directly linked to the success of an export-oriented economy, which relies heavily on women's labor. Thus the political aspect of developmental programs such as "Living Rooms as Factories" and "Mothers' Workshops" is as significant as its material function. In effect, I argue, the satellite factory system is a showcase of the joint interest in women's subordination between the state and the petty capitalists. Besides, as Lucie

Cheng and I have demonstrated in our earlier work, Taiwanese women, like women in other developing countries, are expected to satisfy the sexual appetites of local male customers and international tourists. The KMT state accumulates a substantial amount of capital by tapping into the ever-growing sex industry. The profits of women's sexual labor are seized by the state through taxation and through license fees paid by brothels and by legalized prostitutes (Cheng and Hsiung 1992). Therefore, one must treat the KMT state as a gendered construct, rather than a gender-neutral system as economists and political scientists tend to do.

Third, Gates is right in maintaining that the mode of production involves not only production practices, but also sets of political, social, and ideological relationships that underline the transfer of surpluses from the ruled to the rulers and from the dominated to the dominators. In the case of Taiwan, the KMT state has not only adopted developmental programs to expand the potential labor pool for Taiwan's satellite factories. It has further implemented labor policies that orchestrate a superficially "harmonious" but institutionally oppressive labor regime. Legally, the state has deprived workers in factories with fewer than thirty employees of the right to unionize. Politically, the state gives priority to Taiwan's economic growth over workers' welfare and therefore identifies with the capitalist interest during periods of worker unrest. One significant analytical implication of these policies is that, to capture labor politics in Taiwan's satellite factory system, one needs to go beyond the domain of the conventional, organized, large-scale labor movement. Therefore, in Chapter 6, I draw on ethnographic data to demonstrate the tactics employed by workers to defy the owners' control. I eventually derive sociological concepts from the data that better render the essence of worker resistance.

Finally, and most intriguing, individual households formed the backbone of capitalist development both in premodern China and in postwar Taiwan. This suggests that it is not a historical coincidence that the satellite factory system has figured conspicuously in Taiwan's economic development.

## Class, Gender, and the Satellite Factory System

As I mentioned earlier, the significance of the satellite factory system was not recognized until recent years. Richard Stites' and Stevan Harrell's work on Taiwan's small factories is quite exceptional in this regard. In their first glance at these factories, these researchers were struck by the absence of an organized Taiwanese labor movement and by the diligence of workers in Taiwan under exploitative conditions (Stites 1982, 1985; Harrell 1985). As Stites says, "[Taiwanese] workers viewed extraordinary demands [placed on them by the employers] with an equanimity that would have been embarrassing to an American unionist" (Stites 1985, 234). Harrell records that the families and their hired workers in his field setting "worked from 9:00 or 10:00 in the morning until after midnight" (Harrell 1985, 204). To interpret the exploitative aspects of the small-scale factory operation, researchers have resorted to the notion of entrepreneurship. Stites uses the concept "entrepreneurial strategy" to explain why factory workers in Taiwan are willing to submit to extraordinary demands, including low pay, long working hours, and hazardous working conditions. According to Stites, workers in Taiwan usually consider their factory employment as a transitional stage to becoming employers themselves. "To eschew the opportunity to work overtime, for example, would be to condemn oneself to a longer term of factory employment" (Stites 1985, 242). Harrell, along the same lines, argues that the image of the tireless Chinese should be understood in the context of a family economy that underlines the so-called "entrepreneurial ethic." According to him, Chinese people will work hard if they perceive long-term benefits in terms of improved material conditions or security for their families (Harrell 1985).[9]

By focusing on the industrious and exploitative aspects of the satellite factory, these researchers initiated the attempt to analyze the unique features of Taiwan's economic development. However, their explanations are based on problematic assumptions. First, Stites' analytical framework makes no distinction between the opportunity the satellite factory system presents to the male workers and that open to female workers. It simply assumes that men and women workers in the small factories endure the hardships for the same reason: to be able to open up their own factory businesses in time. Second, Harrell treats the small factory as a socioeconomic unit and implies that its workforce constitutes a homogeneous group with shared interests. His analysis fails to differentiate the bosses from the workers. Finally, and most important, these studies use the family as the primary unit of analysis without considering its analytical limitations. To a certain extent, employing the family as the basic unit of analysis is fruitful because Chinese society as a whole rests on a family and kinship structure. However, this approach, as represented by the class theorists, fails to recognize, and then to incorporate, gender inequality into its analytical framework.[10] Ignoring possible conflict between the individual and the family, it assumes that individual family members have equal access to resources, equal opportunity to pursue personal interests, and equal power in decision making.

In Chinese society the welfare of individual men and women is closely connected to the socioeconomic position of their families. Because the labor of individual men and women has had its principle value as supporting and maintaining the family, one or two individualistically oriented family members can jeopardize the chances for family mobility (Gates 1987). However, studies that pierce through the mask of a united family find that daughters in Taiwan are frequently sent to the factory to support their brother's continuing education, and that the infanticide rate in China is much higher for females than for males (M. Wolf 1972; Greenhalgh 1985; Aird 1990).

The situation in Taiwan's satellite factory system calls for a dialectical approach in analyzing the relationships between the family and individuals in the family. The traditional household structure remained very strong even in the midst of Taiwan's rapid industrialization, as indicated by the persistence of the stem family (household units consisting of parents, their unmarried children, and one married son with his wife and children) (Freedman et al. 1978; Freedman, Chang, and Sun 1982). Preexisting household structures and kinship networks served instrumental functions that facilitated Taiwan's industrialization and rapid economic growth. The start-up capital of small business relies extensively on family savings and on capital generated through informal networks (Greenhalgh 1988; Weng 1985). Family members, relatives, and others recruited through family and kinship networks form the core labor in small factories (Hu 1982, 1984). Large extended households continue to exist because they turn out to be more successful than small nuclear families in exploring nonagricultural opportunities. For example, in a village in south Taiwan, Cohen found that, by the mid-1960s, 68 percent of the joint families had developed nonagricultural enterprises, while only 36 percent of the stem units had done so (Cohen 1976). Rita Gallin found that there was actually a revival of the traditional extended family in a township in central Taiwan. About 34 percent of the local households were stem or joint families in 1959. By 1979, after industrialization had taken hold in this previously agricultural community, the total of stem and joint families had increased to 55 percent (R. Gallin 1984a).

The extended family is upheld because sharing of some of the household chores by mothers-in-law makes it easier for their daughters-in-law to engage in newly available paid employment in the local community (R. Gallin 1984a, 1984b). Family division is postponed because potential conflicts among conjugal units are mitigated by allowing daughters-in-law to keep their independent earnings (R. Gallin 1984a, 1984b). Married women use their extra income to supplement their husband's income, to buy toys, books, or sweets, or to pay tutorial fees for their children. Many women join an informal rotation credit unit. Their savings are used to renovate the house, to help the husband to start his own business, or to buy large items such as a scooter or stereo set. To them, employment opportunities in the satellite factory system represent the paradox of exploitative multiple responsibilities and liberating potential.

In order to capture the familial basis of the satellite factory system while avoiding the pitfalls of the class theorist's failure to recognize gender inequality, this study treats family and individual as a single unit of analysis. Throughout my research, I constantly shift my emphasis back and forth between the individual woman and the family to which she belongs. I compare and contrast the trajectory of possible upward mobilities between men and women, as well as the ways in which the labor of men and women is utilized to achieve or sustain the socioeconomic status of the family.

My effort to simultaneously explore class formation, gender inequality, and the interplay of class and gender structures distinguishes this project from two recent studies that also focus on the importance of small-scale manufacturers in Taiwan's export industry. Gwo-Shyong Shieh's "Manufacturing 'Bosses': Subcontracting Networks under Dependent Capitalism in Taiwan" (1990) explores the production mechanism of subcontracting networks among Taiwan's satellite factories. Shieh demonstrates how subcontracting is used by entrepreneurs to cut costs, transmit risk, activate the massive reserve labor in local communities, and, ultimately, make Taiwan's export industry competitive in the global market. In meticulous detail he delineates the ways in which the labor of homeworkers is recruited, extracted, and employed by contractors and subcontractors at various levels of the subcontracting chain. His systematic analysis confirms a speculation of previous studies, namely, that the upward and downward mobility between bosses and workers in Taiwan's small-scale business has been relatively fluid (Gates 1987). Shieh argues that the satellite factory system generates "opportunities for workers to set up their own manufacturing workshops" and so reduces the confrontational clashes between bosses and wage workers on the shop floor (Shieh 1990, 2).

Jie-Xuan Chen's "The Economic Structure and Social Characteristics of Taiwan's Small and Medium-Size Enterprises" (1991) explores the interorganizational relationships of Taiwan's small and medium-size enterprises. These enterprises are said to relate to one another on the basis of personal ties, semifamilial bonds, and profit-driven incentives. When setting up their own shops, former workers use their personal connections with previous employers as social capital to secure work orders, while these former employers expand their own businesses by capitalizing on large pools of labor activated by the proliferation of small shops.

The strength of Shieh's study lies in the fact that its analytical insights are grounded on ethnographic data. Chen's work, like that of many sinologists, tends to dwell on the Chineseness of the socioeconomic phenomena investigated. Although the work of Shieh and Chen has advanced our understanding of Taiwan's economic development, it presents a number of problems. First, in spite of their painstaking effort to identify the socioeconomic basis of Taiwan's economic development, these authors, like others before them, fail to analyze the gender dimension of a productive system that has heavily exploited gender inequality to its own advantage. Shieh's work suffers from gender blindness by failing to differentiate between the "opportunities" Taiwan's satellite factory system offers to men and those accorded to women. It does not recognize that although most male skilled workers may have the option for "exit" to become their own bosses, many married women are destined to become the unwaged family workers whose labor is crucial in assisting their husbands to set up a small business (Shieh 1990). In addition, to employ terms such as *boss, plant manager, subcontracting head,* and *homeworker* is to gloss over the reality that most of the bosses, plant managers, and subcontracting heads are men whereas the majority of the homeworkers are married women. Shieh fails to point out that homeworkers' "consent" is manufactured on the basis of capitalist oppression as well as on that of patriarchal coercion. Chen likewise makes no attempt to conceptualize patriarchal norms and practices as one significant dimension of business culture among small and medium-size enterprises in Taiwan. The brotherhood bonds that sustain interunit relationships among business owners and managers, as accurately depicted by Chen, in effect perpetuate job segregation along gender lines. Paternalistic management styles institutionalize the abuses and the arbitrariness that impinge daily on employed workers. Failing to recognize that patriarchal norms and practices have been employed by business owners and managers to consolidate their control over workers in general, and married women in particular, is a major flaw of Chen's study.

The picture these authors present perpetuates the intellectual tradition of making women's experiences virtually invisible by ignoring or marginalizing their existence. Their work is also marred by a defective sampling frame, due in part at least to a failure to recognize its embedded biases. All of Jie-Xuan Chen's 114 informants are men with positions above the managerial level. More than 60 percent of them are presidents, general managers, or chairmen of boards of directors or trustees (J.-X. Chen 1991, 166–68). Shieh gathered data from 48 men and 27 women. While most of the men were owners, partners, or managers, most of the women were workers, homeworkers, or owners' wives (Shieh 1990, 334–36). Pictures relying on data gathered from a disproportionate number of men in managerial positions inevitably present the system as it is seen from the "top" and "center." To rectify the biases embedded in such a presentation, my study interweaves the views of bosses with those of ordinary workers, the experiences of men with those of women, and the struggles between persons at the "center" and those at the "margin." I emphasize the ways in which structural inequality along class and gender lines is transformed and perpetuated. I will take up these issues one by one in the later part of this book. Before then, however, it is necessary for readers to acquire a general understanding of Taiwan's historical, political, and economic background.

# 1 Taiwan's Economic Miracle

## The Land and Its People

Taiwan is an island in the Western Pacific, about 700 miles southwest of Japan, 50 miles north of the Philippines, and 90 miles east of the China coast. Of its area of nearly 36,000 square kilometers, only about one-third is arable. Limited natural resources and a large population made Taiwan an ideal candidate for a labor-intensive export-led economy in the late 1960s and early 1970s, when manufactured goods from the Third World gradually caught on in the global market.

Before people in Taiwan themselves became active players in the global economy, several alien powers had conquered Taiwan in their attempt to build international empires. The Dutch occupied Taiwan from 1624 to 1661 as part of their East Indian empire. In 1895, Taiwan once again became a colony, this time of Japan, which defeated China in the Sino-Japanese War in that year. The Japanese appropriated Taiwan's material and human resources in their ambitious attempt to establish an East Asia Commonwealth with themselves at its head. After Japan was defeated in World War II, Taiwan returned to China.

There are four ethnic groups in Taiwan: the aborigines, the Hakka, the Taiwanese, and the mainlanders. The aborigines, the first inhabitants of the island, are of Malayo-Polynesian descent. There is no consensus on when exactly they moved to Taiwan. Some put their arrival between 5000 B.C. and 2000 B.C. Others believe their migration started in 5000 B.C. and ended only around the eleventh century A.D. The aborigines first lost their independence and predominant role in Taiwan to immigrants from China in the 17th century. They were gradually forced to abandon the plains and

23

withdraw into the mountain regions. Because conditions were unsuitable for growing rice, the sweet potato became the main item in their diet, supplemented by millet, taro, and fish. Under the Dutch and Japanese colonization, the aborigines were marginalized further as natural resources were appropriated from the mountains, and attempts at resistance were followed by mass killings.[1] Since 1948 they have suffered further cultural, economic, and political deprivation. Generally speaking, many aborigines have migrated to the cities since the 1960s, in response to Taiwan's industrialization and as a result of the breakdown of their subsistence economy. In the cities the male aborigines often end up in high-risk manual jobs, such as construction, pelagic fishing, trucking, and packing, while young women are often sold into prostitution.[2]

The Taiwanese and the Hakka are descendants of Hokkien and Hakka speakers who migrated from the Fukien and Canton provinces of China in the seventeenth century. Before Taiwan's economic transformation, the majority of Taiwanese and Hakkas worked in agriculture. Since the 1960s, Taiwanese and Hakkas have successfully explored new opportunities that opened up them as a result of Taiwan's economic development. By 1980, Taiwanese and Hakkas owned and operated approximately 85 percent of the country's small enterprises (Gates 1981).

Mainlanders are the 1,020,000 troops and refugees who arrived in Taiwan with the Nationalist Party between 1947 and 1949, as a consequence of the Chinese Communist Party's takeover in China. After arrive in Taiwan, they remained dominant in the military and civil services. Most mainlanders live either in the inner cities abandoned by the Japanese, in the suburbs, or in hillside settlements on the east coast. In the 1950s and 1960s, their jobs were considered prestigious in part because of the attached benefits that include health insurance coverage, monthly military/government subsidies for utilities, rice, and oil, and special educational subsidies for their children.

Not only does each of these four ethnic groups have its own dialect, but the roughly nine aboriginal tribes also speak different dialects. Relations among these four major ethnic groups have been covertly divisive in the last thirty years.[3] Toward the aborigines, the Taiwanese, Hakka, and mainlanders form a single interest group. In Mandarin, the dialect of the mainlanders, which is also the official language, the aborigines used to be called *Gaoshanzhu,* meaning literally "the mountain tribes" or "the mountain race."[4] The Taiwanese call the aborigines *Whan-a,* meaning "the barbarians." The tension between the mainlanders and the Taiwanese and Hakka majority dates back to the early years of the KMT takeover and has scarcely diminished since then. Seen by others and themselves as outsiders, the mainlanders are normally referred to as *Waishengren* (people from other provinces), as opposed to *Benshengren/Taiwanren* (people of the local/ Taiwan province, including the Taiwanese and Hakka). By 1990, 1.7 percent of the population consisted of aborigines, 15 percent were mainlanders, and the rest Taiwanese and Hakka.

## The Political Background

After World War II people in Taiwan at first expressed great enthusiasm about the return of Taiwan to China. Early joy generated by this "liberation" soon vanished as corrupt mainland officials seized public and private property and stole large stocks of raw materials, while ill-equipped and ill-disciplined soldiers looted rural and commercial areas and killed people and animals. On February 28, 1947, in the "2:28" incident, Taiwanese resentment boiled over after mainland soldiers shot a woman peddler accused of selling cigarettes illegally. This incident, concealed by the KMT and treated as political taboo until the mid-1980s, provoked popular uprisings throughout the island. Recent investigations estimate that between 2,000 and 20,000 Taiwanese/Hakka were killed or imprisoned by troops under KMT commander Chen Yi. Most of those killed were elites and local community leaders.

For the next three decades, the KMT viewed Taiwan as a province of China and continued to claim sovereignty over the mainland. It considered itself in a state of war with the communist regime. The KMT in Taiwan has sought to sustain rapid economic progress, to maintain absolute political control, and to reclaim Communist China through military action. In consequence, people in Taiwan have had to bear the economic burden of financing a large military establishment and the political burden in living under an authoritarian government that kept the country in a continuous state of war, restricted individual freedoms, and subjected individuals to arbitrary abuse from military personnel and the police.

Until recently, the Hakka and Taiwanese have been disproportionately disadvantaged because the KMT distrusted and excluded them from the bureaucracy. For almost forty years, the KMT ran elections with virtually no challenges from opposition forces. The overbearing attributes of state policy on labor relations and the state's sweeping command over developmental programs demonstrate the dominance of the KMT. The Democratic Progressive Party (hereafter DPP), the current opposition party, started as a grassroots movement in the mid-1970s. The DPP

only gained official recognition in 1986. After the KMT abandoned martial law in 1987, the DPP gradually gained legitimacy as the main chal-
lenger to KMT rule. It has consolidated its political power by drawing a
distinction between the oppressed *Benshengren* (Taiwanese and Hakka)
and the oppressor *Waishengren* (mainlanders). Even though its political
doctrine mainly represents the interests of middle-class entrepreneurs, the
DPP appeals to various classes of *Benshengren*, all of whom have been excluded from political power under the KMT.

## The Economic Background

Many researchers attribute Taiwan's rapid economic growth to
the infrastructure built by the Japanese during the colonial era. In order
to ensure control over the transport of agricultural surpluses, the Japanese made strategic investments in transport and communication. They
also invested to raise health and sanitation standards so as to improve the
productivity of the local population. Lower mortality rates and steady
growth in population were often cited as the positive side effects of
Japanese colonization. During the colonial era, Taiwan was both a supplier to the Japanese market and a consumer of Japanese goods. Farms for
commercial crops such as tea, pineapples, and sugarcane, along with
the related processing industries, expanded to subsidize Japan's industrialization process. Taiwan's dependent status intensified when specific types
of local industry were suppressed so that Japan might remain the sole
supplier of primary materials such as fertilizer and textiles. Even when
Taiwan was gradually industrialized in the later years of Japanese colonization, the economy was organized to meet the strategic needs of Japan
as it used military force to expand in the Pacific. During World War II,
Japanese policy was expressly designed to prevent Taiwanese entrepreneurs from participating in the industrial sector. When the KMT took
over, Taiwan was therefore still an agricultural economy.

Between 1949 and 1953, the KMT undertook major programs that
dramatically altered the productive structure and social basis of agriculture.
The land reform program reduced farm rents to a maximum of 37.5 percent of the annual yield of the major crop, sold public land to farm families, and limited land ownership to a maximum of three chia (2.9 hectares);
any excessive land was confiscated by the government and redistributed
among tenant families. These measures converted Taiwan's land tenancy
system into one relying primarily on owner-cultivators and, correspond-
ingly, drastically reduced the proportion of tenants (Thorbecke 1979).

The economic implications of the land reform were mixed. Undoubtedly, it redistributed wealth between landlords and tenants. Samuel P.S. Ho (1978) estimates that the average tenant who became an owner-cultivator experienced an income increase of more than 100 percent. The wealth of absentee landlords, meanwhile, was substantially reduced because compensation for their confiscated land was considerably under the market value. Ho calculates a net wealth-redistribution effect of the land reform, measured at 1952 prices, of NT $2.2 billion, or approximately 13 percent of Taiwan's GDP. Another result was that approximately 22 percent of the capital relinquished from the land was reinvested in the nonagricultural sector. This reinvestment ultimately served an important function for Taiwan's economic development. After the land was redistributed, Taiwan's agriculture was in the hands of a large number of very small owners. The average landholding per farm family dropped from 1.29 hectares to 1.05 hectares. The agricultural surplus labor, especially of those families with less than a hectare of land, supplied the manufacturing sector as Taiwan began to engage in labor-intensive export-led growth (Thorbecke 1979). Politically, land reform proved to be a big success for the KMT, for it did not demand immediate sacrifices from its members, yet eliminated potential resistance from the Taiwanese elite and landlord class, extended KMT control to local communities by removing previous power holders, and won support from the tenants and the working class who comprised the majority of the population.

In the 1950s the KMT made every effort to replace imports of nondurable consumer goods (textiles, apparel, wood and leather products) with domestic products. This stage soon ended after Taiwan's limited domestic markets were saturated. The government then initiated major changes to improve the investment climate, liberalize trade and industry, and encourage export-oriented economic growth. The decade of the 1960s was characterized by rapid expansion of the manufacturing sector and by Taiwan's active participation in international markets.

## Economic Transformation and the Export-Led Economy

Within three decades, Taiwan was transformed from an agricultural economy to an industrial economy. Agriculture, which contributed about 30 percent of the domestic product in the early 1960s, had dropped to 6 percent in 1986 (see Table 1.1). The share of agricultural exports in total exports also dropped dramatically, from approximately 91 percent

TABLE 1.1

Gross Domestic Product by Industry, Taiwan, 1960–86 (percent)

| | 1960 | 1965 | 1970 | 1975 | 1980 | 1985 | 1986 |
|---|---|---|---|---|---|---|---|
| Agriculture[a] | 29 | 24 | 16 | 13 | 8 | 6 | 6 |
| Mining[b] | 3 | 4 | 3 | 4 | 3 | 5 | 5 |
| Manufacturing industry | 22 | 26 | 34 | 37 | 42 | 41 | 43 |
| Construction | 4 | 4 | 4 | 5 | 6 | 4 | 4 |
| Retail[c] | 16 | 16 | 15 | 13 | 13 | 14 | 14 |
| Transport[d] | 5 | 5 | 6 | 6 | 6 | 6 | 6 |
| Other[e] | 21 | 21 | 22 | 22 | 22 | 24 | 22 |
| Total | 100 | 100 | 100 | 100 | 100 | 100 | 100 |

[a]Includes hunting, forestry, and fishing.
[b]Includes quarrying and utilities.
[c]Includes wholesale trade.
[d]Includes storage and communication.
[e]Includes banking, insurance, real estate, ownership of dwellings, public administration, and defense and other services.
SOURCE: Bureau of Statistics, Directorate-General of Budget, Accounting, and Statistics (DGBAS), Executive Yuan, Republic of China (1987), Table 26, p. 97.

in 1951–53 to 17 percent in 1971–73 (Thorbecke 1979). In contrast, manufacturing, which accounted for about 25 percent of the domestic product in the early 1960s, increased to 43 percent by 1986.

The shift to manufacturing was accompanied by significant export-led economic growth. In the late 1950s new economic policies encouraged the export expansion that eventually became the source of the economic miracle. The magnitude of this change can be shown from the contribution of exports to GNP. In 1952 exports accounted for only 9 percent of GNP, but rose to 17 percent and 29 percent in 1965 and 1970, respectively. By 1981 exports accounted for fully 53 percent of GNP. This transition can also be shown by comparing the relative importance of domestic and export expansion to output growth. From 1955 to 1961 the contributions of domestic and export expansion to output growth were 61.6 percent and 22.5 percent, respectively, but by 1976 the proportions had changed to 34.7 percent versus 67.7 percent (S. Kuo 1983). One result was that Taiwan became enmeshed in the international market. As measured by the sum of exports plus imports divided by gross domestic product, Taiwan's trade dependency registered over 100 percent in 1979 and has since remained at that level (except in 1982) (Myers 1986).

Besides the transition from agriculture to manufacturing and the export-oriented nature of development, two features distinguish Taiwan's economic experience during the last thirty years. First, Taiwan's export-led growth is based on a dual market structure: the export market is filled with small labor-intensive producers, whereas large capital-intensive producers monopolize the domestic market (T.-C. Chou 1985).[5] Second, Taiwan's industrialization has been decentralized, a phenomenon that is also known as rural industrialization (Hu 1979; Myer 1986).[6]

Since the late 1960s and early 1970s, anthropologists have seen small-scale factories sprout along the newly constructed country roads and in the villages (Arrigo 1980; Diamond 1969; R. Gallin 1984a, 1984b; Hu 1979, 1982). Such small-scale factories were at the core of Taiwan's manufacturing sector throughout the 1970s and 1980s (see Tables 1.2 and 1.3). About 85 percent of all establishments employed fewer than thirty workers, and most—though a declining percentage over the period— had fewer than ten workers. Moreover, the percentage of manufacturing wage workers employed by small establishments increased from 20 percent to 27 percent between 1971 and 1986. In the same period, factories with more than 100 workers never exceeded 5 percent of the total, and the proportion of manufacturing workers they employed decreased by about 15 percent. These statistics are derived from the industrial and commercial census, which only collects and reports information on registered factories. Because the majority of the underground factories are small, their actual number and that of the wage workers in them are underreported and therefore underestimated. Labor statistic show that, in 1987, 40.6 percent of wage workers were employed in factories with fewer than thirty workers (Shieh 1990, 19). To put the point another way, over the last decades, although the percentage of factories with fewer than ten workers decreased, the percentage of manufacturing workers employed in them increased slightly, and the percentage employed in all factories with fewer than thirty workers increased dramatically. Since unions are not allowed in factories with fewer than thirty workers, the increase means that, as industrialization proceeded, the percentage of workers employed in factories where union organization is illegal increased disproportionately.

TABLE 1.2
Percentage Distribution of Factories by Size, Manufacturing, 1971–86

| Number of Employees | 1971 | 1976 | 1981 | 1986 |
|---|---|---|---|---|
| Less than 10 | 68.2 | 67.6 | 69.6 | 63.1 |
| 10–29 | 18.5 | 18.3 | 17.2 | 22.2 |
| 30–49 | 4.8 | 4.9 | 4.8 | 5.8 |
| 50–99 | 3.8 | 4.3 | 4.2 | 4.7 |
| 100–499 | 3.9 | 4.2 | 3.7 | 3.6 |
| 500+ | 0.8 | 0.7 | 0.5 | 0.4 |
| Total number of factories | 44,092 | 72,237 | 94,546 | 118,755 |

SOURCES: 1971: DGBAS, (1972), Table 9, p. 54; 1976: DGBAS (1977), Table 27, pp. 766–76; 1981: Directorate-General of Budget, Accounting, and Statistics, Executive Yuan (1982), Table 71, pp. 490–91; 1986: DGBAS and CEPD (1988), Table 51, pp. 514–15.

TABLE 1.3
Percentage Distribution of Workers Engaged by Factory Size, Manufacturing, 1971–86

| Number of Employees | 1971 | 1976 | 1981 | 1986 |
|---|---|---|---|---|
| Less than 10 | 9.5 | 10.1 | | 11.0 |
| 10–29 | 10.5 | 10.8 | 23.5[a] | 16.0 |
| 30–49 | 6.4 | 6.7 | | 9.6 |
| 50–99 | 9.2 | 11.0 | 52.5[b] | 14.2 |
| 100–499 | 28.3 | 30.2 | | 30.8 |
| 500+ | 36.1 | 31.3 | 24.1 | 18.4 |
| Total number of workers | 1,201,539 | 1,907,581 | 2,178,191 | 2,729,546 |

[a]Less than 29.
[b]Between 30 and 499.
SOURCES: 1971: Ho (1978, 378); 1976: DGBAS (1977), Table 20, p. 426; 1981: Directorate-General of Budget, Accounting, and Statistics, Executive Yuan, 1982, Table 39, p. 318; 1986: DGBAS (1988), Table 44, p. 428.

The uniqueness of Taiwan's experience becomes clearer when we compare it to its neighbor, South Korea. In 1976 the average size of the Taiwanese factory (34.6 employees) was only half that of the average Korean factory (68.8 employees) (Scitovsky 1986, 146). If Taiwanese and Korean factories with less than five employees had been included, the contrast would have been even greater.[7] Korea's four largest manufacturing concerns contributed 45 percent of the GNP in 1985, while in Taiwan, the five largest firms contributed only 5.45 percent (Hamilton and Biggart 1988). Although it is hard to estimate the exact number of small factories in Taiwan, since many of them either never register as factories or operate illegally, government figures have shown a persistent increase in the number of factories, combined with limited growth of the average size of the factories over time. Between 1966 and 1976 the number of factories increased by 150 percent, while average size increased only by 29 percent. In South Korea, the relation between those two changes were reversed: the number of factories increased less than 10 percent, while the size of the factories increased by 176 percent (Scitovsky 1986, 146).

## Craft-Based versus Non–Craft-Based Production

In contrast, Taiwan provides a unique opportunity to illuminate the ongoing debate on flexible competitiveness that Michael Piore and Charles Sabel have initiated in the Italian context (Piore and Sabel 1984). Parallels have frequently been drawn between Italian developments and the Taiwanese "economic miracle" of the last two decades (Orru 1991; *The Economist* 1993). The similarities between Taiwan and Italy are indeed striking when we look at the rapid growth of their economies. Instead of relying upon a small number of large corporations, the economies of both these countries are dominated by small and medium-size family enterprises producing for an international market (Orru 1991). By 1987, Italy had become the fifth-largest economy in the Western world, its GDP having grown at a higher rate than that of most European economies from 1978 to 1987. Taiwan's economic progress has been equally impressive. Its GNP has doubled since 1986. By 1989, Taiwan was the second-richest country (after Japan) in terms of foreign exchange reserves and the world's thirteenth-largest trading partner.

Piore and Sabel attribute Italy's success to that country's craft-based economy. In their analytical paradigm, they delineate two models of industrial development: the mass-production model using special-purpose machines and semiskilled workers to turn out standardized products, and the craft-based model in which skilled workers use general-purpose machines to produce a wide range of goods to accommodate a constantly fluctuating market. In theory, craft-based production is superior to mass production because, by manufacturing specialized products, it can respond more flexibly to fluctuating market demand. The adaptability of craft production rests on "permanent technological innovation," under a production strategy that Piore and Sabel call "flexible specialization." This craft-based flexibility is fostered at several levels. At the community level, formal institutions, such as the municipal government or a confederation of firms, are responsible for ensuring that competition among firms will not take the form of price and wage reduction, but instead will be continued through technological innovation. Within the firm, institutional practices, such as profit sharing and cooperation between capital and labor, encourage skilled workers to innovate and to help reorganize plant operations to meet the constantly changing market. The predominant norms governing labor relations between capitalists and workers are cooperation and solidarity. Rather than relying upon organized unions, disputes in craft-based firms are resolved through substantive resolution.

In Taiwan, manufacturers have dealt with uncertainty and fluctuations in the global market by developing rather different operational practices and managerial logic than have emerged in Italy. Instead of engaging in permanent technological innovation created by skilled workers, Taiwan's satellite factory system mitigates structural uncertainty through the utilization of a large group of married women who endure their multiple responsibilities at work and in the home "flexibly." What I would characterize as non-craft-based flexibility achieves its competitive edge in a highly unstable international market not through the collaboration of capital and labor, but through a combination of managerial tactics and paternalistic control that maximizes the level of productivity while minimizing the workers' discontent. This oppressive labor regime is fostered by a particular sociopolitical environment that fragments worker resistance.

A systematic comparison between the Italian craft-based paradigm and the non-craft-based paradigm represented by Taiwan's satellite factory system yields a number of interesting results. First, in the craft-based paradigm described by Piore and Sabel, subcontracting is a strategy to encourage technological innovation and, consequently, flexible specialization. Production is divided into discrete tasks that are carried out by small, specialized firms. A merchant-manufacturer usually coordinates the production and assembles the final product. In the non-craft-based production characteristic of Taiwan's satellite factory system, however, subcontracting is used to cut overhead, lower labor costs, transfer risk, and mitigate the effects of fluctuations in demand. Factories either reduce their reliance on permanent full-time workers by hiring casual and piece-rate workers through subcontracting, or they subcontract out their work to sweatshops and homeworkers.

Second, unlike Italy, Taiwan's competitive flexibility is based on fluid networks of small firms that emerge and die in response to fluctuating market demand. In Taiwan, skilled workers open their own shops to escape their proletarian status (Shieh 1990), while successful businessmen tend to spread their risk and deal with uncertainty by engaging in different lines of business (Hamilton and Biggart 1988). These phenomena can best be described as follows:

> Most of the small and medium businesses are like desert plants. When the rain falls, they suck up every drop. They bloom, blossom, and then die rapidly. When rain falls next time at a different location, a new group of plants goes through the same cycle. It is impossible to find long lasting, well grounded big trees/business in this case. (Chen and Qiu 1984; 478–79)

Taiwan's satellite factory system, therefore, provides a foundation for hypercompetitiveness in international markets.

Third, because the craft-based firms of Italy and Spain produce luxury goods, experimental products, specialized equipment used in mass production, and standardized goods where market demand is unstable, they rely heavily upon research and development. The products of non-craft-based factories in Taiwan require very little research and development. They seize economic niches in the global market previously filled by goods produced in the First World. In fact, in a recent study Lucie Cheng and Gary Gereffi find that garment makers in Italy, France, the United Kingdom, and Japan supply products to designers' stores in the United States, while Taiwan, South Korea, Hong Kong, and Singapore sell their products to the second or third level of retailers, that is, stores such as Kmart, Wal-Mart, Sears, and Target (Cheng and Gereffi 1994).

Fourth, the operational mechanism of craft-based production is nonunionized and decentralized. Skilled workers play significant roles in management and in research and development, and they share in the profits. The operational mechanism of non-craft-based production is also nonunionized, but it is centralized and authoritarian. In Taiwan, small family business is highly intolerant of different opinions, shows minimal concern for the employees' welfare, and scores at the bottom on open communication between management and employees (K.-L. Huang 1984).[8] The owner's authority and power are institutionalized and un-challengeable. Workers have little say in management.

## The Changing Economic Role of Women

Viewed from the perspective of gender, it is striking how mar-kedly the employment experiences of men and women differed as the economic focus shifted from agriculture to manufacturing. One area where Taiwan experienced the economic transformation most strongly was in female employment. In 1970 about half the employed female pop-ulation worked in agriculture; but as the agricultural sector declined, the number of women on the farm decreased to one-third in 1975 and to only one-tenth in 1987 (see Table 1.4). By contrast, agriculture absorbed only about one-third of the employed male population in 1970; by 1987 slightly less than one-fifth of male workers were still employed in this sector.

Within a period of ten years, manufacturing replaced agriculture as the sector where the greatest proportion of women were employed. In 1970 less than one-fifth (18.6 percent) of female workers were em-ployed in manufacturing. By 1987 the figure had jumped to 41.5 per-cent. For males, however, manufacturing absorbed a little more than one-seventh (13.7 percent) of the employed population in 1970 and only reached 31.7 percent in 1987.

The changes in employment distribution across industries shows that the largest outflow occurred in agriculture, while the largest inflow occurred in manufacturing (see Table 1.5). This generalization was true for both male and female workers. However, the magnitude of the over-all changes was greater for females than for males. As the figures for agri-culture show, in the ten-year period, there was a decline of about 50 per-cent for females, as against a decline of less than 20 percent for males. In the same period, the number of women in manufacturing increased more than 80 percent, the number of men by 60 percent. The most dramatic

TABLE 1.4

Percentage Distribution of Employed Persons Aged 15 Years and
Over by Industry and Gender, 1970–87

| | 1970 | | 1975 | | 1980 | | 1987 | |
|---|---|---|---|---|---|---|---|---|
| | **M** | **F** | **M** | **F** | **M** | **F** | **M** | **F** |
| Agriculture | 35.1 | 48.4 | 29.0 | 35.5 | 22.1 | 15.7 | 17.2 | 11.8 |
| Mining | 1.4 | 0.6 | 1.2 | 0.4 | 0.6 | 0.2 | 0.5 | 0.2 |
| Manufacturing | 13.7 | 18.6 | 19.6 | 28.8 | 25.2 | 40.2 | 31.7 | 41.5 |
| Utilities | 0.6 | 0.2 | 0.6 | 0.2 | 0.7 | 0.3 | 0.6 | 0.1 |
| Construction | 5.3 | 0.5 | 6.3 | 0.9 | 8.6 | 1.8 | 9.8 | 1.8 |
| Commerce | 10.1 | 11.2 | 10.7 | 13.4 | 11.8 | 15.7 | 16.8 | 19.9 |
| Transportation | 5.9 | 2.0 | 6.2 | 2.3 | 6.7 | 3.0 | 7.7 | 2.2 |
| Finance and Insurance | 1.3 | 1.4 | 1.4 | 1.7 | 1.7 | 3.2 | 2.5 | 3.7 |
| Services | 26.5 | 17.1 | 24.9 | 16.8 | 22.4 | 19.9 | 13.1 | 18.9 |
| Other | 0.0 | 0.0 | 0.0 | 0.0 | 0.0 | 0.0 | — | — |
| Total | 99.9 | 100.0 | 99.9 | 100.0 | 99.8 | 100.0 | 99.9 | 100.1 |

SOURCES: 1970: Census Office of the Executive Yuan (1972, 226–28); 1975: Census Office of the Executive Yuan (1977, 45–46); 1980: Census Office of the Executive Yuan (1982, 272–73); 1987: DGBAS (1988), Table 6, p. 10.

change in this decade occurred between 1975 and 1980. For females, the drop in agricultural employment was 300 percent, while the increase in manufacturing was 223.23 percent. For males, however, the decrease in agriculture was only 19.5 percent, while the increase in manufacturing industry was a mere 59.2 percent. In sum, the magnitude of outflow was fifteen times greater for female laborers than for male laborers in agriculture, while the magnitude of inflow among women was about four times greater than among men in manufacturing.

These data demonstrate that women as a group have been affected by Taiwan's economic transformation much more than men. While manufacturing became a major sector of employment for both men and women, its relative importance was greater for women. By 1987, 41.5 percent of female workers were in manufacturing as against 31.7 percent of male workers. Conversely, a larger proportion of men continued to

TABLE 1.5

Allocation of Changes by Industry and Gender, Taiwan, 1970–80

| | 1970–75 | | 1975–80 | | 1970–80 | |
|---|---|---|---|---|---|---|
| | **M** | **F** | **M** | **F** | **M** | **F** |
| Agriculture | −14.5 | 5.1 | −19.5 | −300.2 | −17.4 | −47.8 |
| Mining | −0.1 | 0.2 | −2.4 | −2.7 | −1.5 | −0.3 |
| Manufacturing | 61.3 | 52.8 | 59.2 | 223.2 | 60.1 | 82.3 |
| Utilities | 1.4 | 0.2 | 1.2 | 1.4 | 1.3 | 0.4 |
| Construction | 13.3 | 2.1 | 22.1 | 15.0 | 18.4 | 4.3 |
| Commerce | 14.8 | 18.4 | 18.5 | 52.8 | 16.9 | 24.3 |
| Transportation | 8.9 | 2.9 | 9.8 | 14.8 | 9.4 | 5.0 |
| Finance and Insurance | 2.0 | 2.3 | 3.4 | 26.6 | 2.8 | 6.6 |
| Services | 13.1 | 16.0 | 7.6 | 69.0 | 9.9 | 25.2 |
| Other | −0.1 | .0 | .0 | .0 | −0.1 | .0 |
| Total | 100.1 | 100.0 | 99.9 | 99.9 | 99.8 | 100.0 |
| N = | 514,609 | 501,316 | 697,545 | 104,952 | 1,212,163 | 606,357 |

SOURCES: 1970: Census Office of the Executive Yuan (1972, 226–28); 1975: Census Office of the Executive Yuan (1977, 45–46); 1980: Census Office of the Executive Yuan (1982, 272–73).

work in agriculture which, by 1980, employed only a handful of female workers.

Taiwan's export-led growth and the incorporation of its economy into the global market have been mixed blessings for women. Although women have had a chance to explore newly available employment opportunities, the changes have rendered them structurally vulnerable and subject to exploitation. As manufacturing has become the major component of Taiwan's export-led growth, women as a group have supplied the essential labor. A higher proportion of women than of men worked on the production lines. In response to Taiwan's economic transformation, women virtually abandoned farmwork. This change rendered them particularly vulnerable, because unlike men, they could no longer rely on employment in agriculture as a backup in times of economic recession. Despite all these changes, however, one thing remained the same:

TABLE 1.6

Percentage of Males and Females Aged 15 and Over Employed in Agriculture, 1970–80

| Age | 1970 M | 1970 F | 1975 M | 1975 F | 1980 M | 1980 F |
|---|---|---|---|---|---|---|
| 15–19 | 45.3 | 40.9 | 30.9 | 22.1 | 16.0 | 5.5 |
| 20–24 | 21.6 | 35.5 | 15.2 | 20.7 | 8.8 | 5.7 |
| 25–29 | 34.2 | 46.1 | 23.2 | 28.8 | 15.3 | 9.2 |
| 30–34 | 38.1 | 55.5 | 26.6 | 40.2 | 17.6 | 15.6 |
| 35–39 | 36.9 | 59.5 | 33.4 | 47.9 | 23.5 | 24.1 |
| 40–44 | 29.2 | 58.3 | 34.7 | 54.7 | 31.5 | 32.3 |
| 45–49 | 29.3 | 59.4 | 29.2 | 59.1 | 33.9 | 41.5 |
| 50–54 | 37.1 | 63.8 | 31.2 | 60.5 | 29.3 | 46.3 |
| 55–59 | 45.3 | 64.8 | 41.3 | 65.0 | 31.1 | 48.4 |
| 60–64 | 56.1 | 64.0 | 51.9 | 67.2 | 41.9 | 54.1 |
| 65+ | 61.5 | 58.3 | 64.6 | 60.8 | 54.9 | 54.8 |

SOURCES: 1970: Census Office of the Executive Yuan (1972, 226–28); 1975: Census Office of the Executive Yuan (1977, 45–46); 1980: Census Office of the Executive Yuan (1982, 272–73).

Women continued to be concentrated in a single economic sector—agriculture in 1970, manufacturing in 1980.

Another gender-specific aspect of the shift from agriculture to manufacturing has been the changing age distribution of the Taiwanese female workforce. Women's involvement in agriculture is positively correlated with their age; that is, older women are more likely to work in agriculture than younger women (see Table 1.6). The employment outflow in agriculture occurred first among younger women and then trickled down to women of older cohorts. In 1970 about 40 percent of women aged 15 to 19 were employed in agriculture. By the time they reached 20 to 24, only about 20 percent of them still worked in agriculture. For the other cohorts, the decreases were all smaller than 10 percent during the same period. From 1975 to 1980, in contrast, the largest outflow occurred among women who were 20 to 34, indicating that as industrialization proceeded, more married women entered the nontraditional sector.

TABLE 1.7

Percentage of Males and Females Aged 15 and Over Employed in Manufacturing, 1970–80

| Age | 1970 | | 1975 | | 1980 | |
|---|---|---|---|---|---|---|
| | M | F | M | F | M | F |
| 15–19 | 24.4 | 34.9 | 36.1 | 55.2 | 45.1 | 67.9 |
| 20–24 | 10.6 | 22.8 | 17.0 | 37.8 | 21.0 | 49.0 |
| 25–29 | 19.5 | 11.8 | 27.9 | 20.2 | 34.2 | 32.7 |
| 30–34 | 16.1 | 9.4 | 23.7 | 15.6 | 29.5 | 25.7 |
| 35–39 | 12.9 | 9.2 | 19.0 | 14.8 | 24.8 | 26.0 |
| 40–44 | 10.0 | 8.1 | 15.6 | 12.5 | 20.2 | 24.4 |
| 45–49 | 9.8 | 7.6 | 12.5 | 10.7 | 16.9 | 20.4 |
| 50–54 | 9.8 | 6.5 | 14.0 | 8.6 | 17.4 | 16.3 |
| 55–59 | 9.0 | 6.6 | 12.5 | 7.8 | 17.6 | 13.7 |
| 60–64 | 7.6 | 6.8 | 8.6 | 6.9 | 13.1 | 10.1 |
| 65+ | 5.6 | 8.3 | 6.1 | 7.8 | 9.5 | 8.5 |

SOURCES: 1970: Census Office of the Executive Yuan (1972, 226–28); 1975: Census Office of the Executive Yuan (1977, 45–46); 1980: Census Office of the Executive Yuan (1982, 272–73).

The effects of economic transformation on men do not have a strong age dimension. Although men aged 65 and older have the highest level of involvement in agriculture, the differences for other age groups do not show any systematic pattern. Young men were as likely as middle-aged men to be involved in agriculture. Nor does the percentage decrease of males employed in agriculture show a systematic, strong negative correlation with age. Although young males had a higher outflow level from 1970 to 1975 than did middle-aged and older males, from 1975 to 1980 the degree of outflow was similar across age groups.

Contrary to the patterns in agriculture, the level of women's involvement in manufacturing is negatively correlated with their age. The younger the woman, the more likely she is to be working in manufacturing industry (see Table 1.7). In 1970, 1975, and 1980, women aged 29 or younger had the highest level of employment in this sector. However, middle-aged women had the highest rate of increase, higher than both younger and older women. From 1970 to 1980, the percentage of women aged 25 to 49 in manufacturing almost tripled. Between 1975 and 1980, the involvement in manufacturing of women aged 40 to 54 doubled. Men's level of employment in manufacturing is also negatively correlated with age.[9] However, there is almost no difference in the degree of change between men in the middle-aged and younger groups.

Several differences stand out when we compare the effects of Taiwan's economic transformation on men and women, taking the age factor into consideration. First of all, the age structure plays a much more significant role in mediating these effects for the female population than for the male population. In agriculture, women of older cohorts have a higher level of involvement and are less likely to leave the sector than women of younger cohorts. In the manufacturing sector, however, the relationship is reversed: younger women have a higher level of involvement and are more likely to join the sector. In contrast, the age structure has relatively limited effects on men. It plays a role in the manufacturing sector, but not in agriculture.

Because of the mediating effects of age, women of the youngest cohorts were the first to leave the agricultural sector. They were also the first drawn into the manufacturing sector. However, it is the middle-aged women who had the highest rate of increase in their involvement in manufacturing over the ten-year period. The fact that Taiwan has a high marriage rate (more than 90 percent of women over age 35 were married in 1983) makes it necessary to bring women's marital status into the picture.

As in many other countries, married women in Taiwan are much less likely to be in paid employment than single women. However, over the last two decades, the gap has narrowed: the percentage of married women in the labor market increased significantly, while the participation rate of single women declined. By 1988, 42.7 percent of married women were in the job market (see Table 1.8). The percentage distribution of the female employed population by marital status shows that the majority of the employed women are married; and the share of married women continues to grow (see Table 1.9). Married women have contributed the largest proportion of the 250 percent increase in the female employed population over the last two decades (see Table 1.10).

The differing implications of Taiwan's export-led economy for men and women can be further demonstrated by comparing their employment status. In selected major industries, the proportion of male employers exceeds that of their female counterparts, while among unpaid family workers, women consistently outnumber men (see Tables 1.11 and 1.12). Statistics also show that in the manufacturing sector, the per-

TABLE 1.8
Female Labor Force Participation Rate by Marital Status,
Selected Years

|  | 1967 | 1973 | 1984 | 1988 |
|---|---|---|---|---|
| Single | 57.3 | 62.3 | 58.5 | 54.6 |
| Married | 27.2 | 35.3 | 39.0 | 42.7 |
| Divorced/widowed | 18.9 | 19.3 | 23.1 | 25.6 |

SOURCES: 1967–84: Liu Yu-lan (1985, 24); 1988: DGBAS and CEPD (1989), Table 1, p. 2.

TABLE 1.9
Percentage of Employed Women by Marital Status, Selected Years

|  | 1967 | 1973 | 1984 | 1988 |
|---|---|---|---|---|
| Single | 40.9 | 43.7 | 39.4 | 34.5 |
| Married | 53.0 | 51.7 | 55.8 | 60.2 |
| Divorced/widowed | 6.2 | 4.7 | 4.8 | 5.3 |
| Total percentage | 100.1 | 100.1 | 100.0 | 100.0 |
| Total number | 1,207,000 | 1,867,000 | 2,713,000 | 2,986,000 |

SOURCES: Same as Table 1.8.

TABLE 1.10
Sources of Changes in Female Employment, by Marital Status,
Selected Years

|  | 1967–73 | 1973–84 | 1984–88 | 1967–88 |
|---|---|---|---|---|
| Single | 48.6 | 30.1 | − 14.3 | 22.0 |
| Married | 49.2 | 65.0 | 103.3 | 65.0 |
| Divorced/widowed | 2.2 | 4.9 | 11.0 | 4.8 |
| Total percentage | 100.0 | 100.0 | 100.0 | 100.0 |
| Total number | 660,000 | 846,000 | 273,000 | 1,779,000 |

SOURCES: 1967–84: Liu Yu-lan (1985, 22); 1988: DGBAS and CEPD (1989), Table 9, p. 20.

TABLE 1.11

Percentage Distribution of Women and Men as Employers,
Selected Industries, 1966–86

|      |     | Agriculture | | Manufacturing | | Commerce | | Services | |
|------|-----|------|------|------|------|------|------|------|------|
|      |     | M | F | M | F | M | F | M | F |
| 1966 | (a) | 0.9 | 0.3 | 5.4 | 1.7 | 5.6 | 1.5 | 3.7 | 3.0 |
|      | (b) | 89.4 | 10.6 | 89.3 | 10.7 | 89.9 | 10.1 | 70.9 | 29.1 |
| 1971 | (a) | 0.9 | 0.1 | 6.7 | 0.9 | 7.3 | 1.8 | 4.3 | 2.4 |
|      | (b) | 97.6 | 2.4 | 92.5 | 7.5 | 88.7 | 11.3 | 74.3 | 25.7 |
| 1976 | (a) | 0.6 | 0.1 | 5.9 | 0.7 | 6.4 | 2.2 | 3.1 | 2.0 |
|      | (b) | 90.3 | 9.7 | 92.7 | 7.3 | 85.3 | 14.7 | 73.2 | 26.8 |
| 1981 | (a) | 1.6 | 0.8 | 8.5 | 0.7 | 11.5 | 2.9 | 4.6 | 2.6 |
|      | (b) | 82.4 | 17.7 | 94.5 | 5.3 | 86.8 | 13.2 | 72.2 | 27.8 |
| 1986 | (a) | 1.8 | 0.5 | 8.2 | 0.6 | 10.6 | 2.4 | 4.8 | 2.0 |
|      | (b) | 88.9 | 11.1 | 94.5 | 5.5 | 85.7 | 14.3 | 74.4 | 25.6 |

(a) Proportion of total employed males/females who are employers.
(b) Proportion of total employers who are males/females.
SOURCE: B. Chou (1989, 450–57).

TABLE 1.12

Percentage Distribution of Women and Men as Unpaid Family
Workers, Selected Industries, 1966–86

|      |     | Agriculture | | Manufacturing | | Commerce | | Services | |
|------|-----|------|------|------|------|------|------|------|------|
|      |     | M | F | M | F | M | F | M | F |
| 1966 | (a) | 28.7 | 74.9 | 4.4 | 12.1 | 8.3 | 41.6 | 2.0 | 7.2 |
|      | (b) | 48.8 | 51.2 | 48.6 | 51.4 | 31.9 | 68.1 | 34.9 | 65.1 |
| 1971 | (a) | 23.0 | 73.9 | 2.8 | 9.7 | 8.2 | 43.2 | 2.0 | 5.7 |
|      | (b) | 38.4 | 61.6 | 32.3 | 67.7 | 27.0 | 73.0 | 36.5 | 63.5 |
| 1976 | (a) | 20.9 | 71.4 | 2.5 | 4.7 | 6.6 | 36.3 | 1.3 | 4.6 |
|      | (b) | 38.0 | 62.0 | 44.6 | 55.4 | 26.5 | 73.5 | 34.2 | 65.8 |
| 1981 | (a) | 16.1 | 65.8 | 2.4 | 4.6 | 6.2 | 36.3 | 1.4 | 5.2 |
|      | (b) | 37.1 | 62.9 | 43.1 | 56.9 | 22.0 | 78.0 | 28.6 | 71.4 |
| 1986 | (a) | 16.5 | 67.3 | 1.9 | 5.3 | 6.6 | 36.3 | 1.4 | 5.8 |
|      | (b) | 34.7 | 65.3 | 30.7 | 69.3 | 19.9 | 80.1 | 22.5 | 77.5 |

(a) Proportion of total employed males/females who are unpaid.
(b) Proportion of total unpaid workers who are male/female.
SOURCE: B. Chou (1989, 450–57).

TABLE 1.13

Percentage Distribution of Employment Status for Men and Women in Manufacturing, 1966–86

|  | 1966 | 1971 | 1976 | 1981 | 1986 |
|---|---|---|---|---|---|
| **Male** | | | | | |
| Employers | 5.4 | 7.0 | 5.9 | 8.5 | 8.2 |
| Self-employed workers | 13.7 | 8.5 | 6.8 | 5.6 | 5.5 |
| Unpaid family workers | 4.4 | 2.3 | 2.5 | 2.4 | 1.9 |
| Paid workers | | | | | |
|   Private | 58.5 | 71.8 | 75.8 | 77.0 | 79.5 |
|   Government | 17.9 | 10.2 | 9.0 | 6.5 | 4.9 |
| Total | 99.9 | 99.8 | 100.0 | 100.0 | 100.0 |
| **Female** | | | | | |
| Employers | 1.7 | 0.9 | 0.7 | 0.7 | 0.6 |
| Self-employed workers | 12.8 | 2.6 | 1.3 | 1.0 | 0.9 |
| Unpaid family workers | 12.1 | 9.7 | 4.7 | 4.6 | 5.3 |
| Paid workers | | | | | |
|   Private | 67.1 | 83.6 | 91.1 | 92.2 | 92.2 |
|   Government | 6.3 | 3.2 | 2.3 | 1.5 | 1.0 |
| Total | 100.0 | 100.0 | 100.1 | 100.0 | 100.0 |

SOURCE: B. Chou (1989, 452).

centage of the male workforce classified as employers has increased over time, while the percentage for females has decreased (see Table 1.11). This decrease in percentage does not imply a decline in the absolute number of female owners, because the total number of female workers has increased dramatically; but the figure does suggest that Taiwan's export-led economy has created many opportunities for men to become employers, while the new opportunities open to women are mainly as wage workers.

In the 1960s, the majority of working women not hired as wage laborers were self-employed and unpaid family workers (see Table 1.13). Unfortunately, no statistical data are available at this point to reveal what kind of work the self-employed women were doing. Anthropological case studies document that women engaged in various income-generating activities. Among other things, they worked as seamstresses, peddlers, hairdressers, storekeepers, and matchmakers (Diamond 1969; B. Gallin 1966; M. Wolf 1972). Two decades later, the majority of them were still unpaid family workers, though the percentage was lower than before. By contrast, nonwaged males were mainly self-employed in 1966, and by 1986 the majority of these males were employers. Few men were ever unpaid family workers.

In addition to the marked difference between men and women in the category of unpaid family worker, one has to keep in mind that the number of female unpaid family workers has very likely been underreported. According to the official definition, in order to be counted as an unpaid family worker, one has to work a minimum of fifteen hours a week. Yet, for an individual to be recorded as an owner, self-employed worker, privately employed worker, or government-employed worker, only a minimum of one hour per week is required. As a result of this bias in the definition of employment categories, many married women who work in a family factory may have been counted as "housewives" instead of being classified as unpaid family workers.

In the manufacturing sector, the proportion of females categorized as employers or as self-employed workers has decreased over time, while the proportion of females described as unpaid family workers has increased (see Table 1.14). In 1966 women made up 51.4 percent of the unpaid family worker category. By 1986 the percentage had increased to 69.3 percent. In contrast, by 1986 about 90 percent of the workers in the top two employment strata in manufacturing industry were men; 94.5 percent of employers were males, and 89.0 percent of self-employed workers were males.

## Conclusions

From the perspective of this study, the statistics in this chapter demonstrate two main characteristics of Taiwan's "economic miracle." First, contrary to the impression given by some of the existing literature, the effect on women of economic development in Taiwan has not been limited to young single women. When large factories were first established in Taiwan's export processing zones in the 1970s, it was primarily single women who were drawn to the assembly line. Since then, however, the growing number of family-oriented factories in local communities have relied largely on the labor of married women. Some of those women were former factory girls who left their jobs in the large firms

TABLE 1.14
Gender and Employment Status (percent) in Manufacturing, 1966–86

| | Employers | | Self-employed Workers | | Unpaid Family Workers | | Private Workers | | Government Workers | |
|---|---|---|---|---|---|---|---|---|---|---|
| | M | F | M | F | M | F | M | F | M | F |
| 1966 | 89.3 | 10.5 | 73.6 | 26.4 | 48.6 | 51.4 | 69.3 | 30.7 | 88.1 | 11.9 |
| 1971 | 92.5 | 7.5 | 84.5 | 15.5 | 32.3 | 67.7 | 58.6 | 41.4 | 83.9 | 16.1 |
| 1976 | 92.7 | 7.3 | 89.2 | 10.9 | 44.7 | 55.4 | 55.8 | 44.2 | 85.5 | 14.2 |
| 1981 | 94.7 | 5.3 | 88.8 | 11.3 | 43.1 | 57.0 | 54.5 | 45.5 | 86.5 | 13.5 |
| 1986 | 94.5 | 5.5 | 89.0 | 11.0 | 30.7 | 69.3 | 52.2 | 47.8 | 85.7 | 14.3 |

SOURCE: B. Chou (1989, 452).

upon marriage. Others were married women who were new to manufacturing production. The increasing importance of this employment sector meant that, in the 1970s and 1980s, the highest rate of increase in female labor force participation, was among married women. By the end of 1980s, in fact, the majority of women in the paid labor force were married.

Second, Taiwan's economic development has differing effects on men and women. A relatively larger percentage of men remained in agriculture, rendering them less vulnerable than women in times of economic recession. At the same time, women did not benefit as much as might have been expected from their heavy involvement in manufacturing industry. Indeed, their position within the manufacturing sector continued to deteriorate. Over the last twenty years, Taiwan's export-led growth has allowed many men to escape proletarianization by becoming bosses. The same period saw a decrease in the proportion of women employers and an increase in the percentage of unpaid female family workers.

In the following chapters I employ ethnographic data to further demonstrate the relationship between class and gender stratification. Even though the stories and experiences I present are those of particular individuals, they depict a larger landscape where women have built, and continue to build, their lives within a system structured around class and gender, and shaped by the operations of capitalism.

# 2

# "Living Rooms as Factories": Women, the State, and Taiwan's Economic Development

$\rm T$he KMT state has been and continues to be a patriarchal state. Its conservatism and antifeminism have been evidence since the KMT came to power in 1927. Even after it fled to Taiwan, the KMT continued to advocate patriarchal values and to sponsor programs and projects that perpetuate women's familial roles. For example, in the 1960s and 1970s, through the Women's Department and the Chinese Women's Anti-Aggression League, a semiofficial organization, middle-class women were encouraged to take part in voluntary activities such as sewing clothing for military personnel and collecting or donating cash, clothes, and food for needy military dependents. At the same time, these women were discouraged from participating in paid employment. Data collected in the late 1960s and early 1970s suggest that the KMT's conservative position has had a profound impact. Younger women who grew up under the KMT regime were less likely to hold paid employment after marriage than women of the older generation who developed their identities in the 1930s when liberalism was prominent (Diamond 1973a, 1973b, 1975).

For working-class women, the lack of adequate welfare services sponsored by the state has made it impossible to attain autonomous status through labor-force participation. Married working-class women seeking outside employment appreciate the extended family because their in-laws can provide much-needed extra help with baby-sitting and family chores. Older women are forced to delay their retirement as new employment opportunities become available to their daughters-in-law. The lack of social security benefits puts older women into a dependent position; their reproductive labor is appropriated in exchange for the daily care they will need in later days. According to Rita Gallin, both young and old women are now compelled to support the patriarchal family system rather than to challenge its legitimacy, even though an increasing number of women are participating in productive labor (R. Gallin 1984b).

In general, scholars contend that women's subordination in Taiwan is not simply a product of traditional values and culture. Instead, it is an outgrowth of patriarchal capitalism, in which the interests of the capitalists,the state, and the international market are all served (Diamond 1973a, 1973b, 1975; R. Gallin 1984a, 1984b; Gates 1979). However, previous studies have not shown concretely how the patriarchal capitalist state has been able to reconcile the potential conflict between the capitalist's interest in having plenty of cheap female labor and the patriarchal demand for the unconditional services of full-time housewives. Nor have they documented precisely where the KMT state stands on the issues of women, family, and labor-force participation in the course of Taiwan's economic development.

## Community Development Programs

Several developmental programs and policies were promulgated by the KMT in response to the export-led economy. In 1968, two years after the first export processing zone was established in Taiwan, the government designed an eight-year Community Development Program, which has been further extended several times since. The program included three substantive areas; basic engineering and construction projects, production and social welfare projects, and ethics and morality enforcement projects. The goals of these projects were threefold: "To extend basic infrastructure into the local community; to diminish poverty and improve civilian life at the community level; and to advocate traditional virtues and reestablish traditional ethics nationwide" (Taiwanshenzhengfu Shehuichu, n.d., 20). Numerous programs and activities to implement these projects have been designed and carried out nationwide and in the local community.[1] From 1968 to 1981 a total of NT$5.9 billion (US$147.5 million) was injected into local communities in the name of these Community Development Programs (Taiwan Shengzhengfu Yanjiu Kaohe Fazhan Weiyuanhui 1983, 14).

The *Keting ji gongchang* or "Living Rooms as Factories" program and the *Mama jiaoshi* or "Mothers' Workshops" were two major Community Development campaigns. They laid out the KMT's plans to incorporate women into productive labor while instructing them to fulfill their moral obligation to promote Taiwan's economic development through their traditional roles in the family as wives, mothers, and caretakers.

The essential purpose of the Mothers' Workshops Program was to promote traditional feminine ethics and family values. As stated by the program's creator, Governor Dong-min Xie, who later became the vice president of the Republic of China:

> The real essence of the program is to educate mothers to help their husbands and teach their children, and to train them to become dutiful wives and loving mothers. It also tends to advocate knowledge of homemaking so that we will positively promote progress, harmony, and solidarity in the family and society. . . . After all, if we have educated a qualified mother, we actually have taken care of a whole family. If every family is being taken care of, the whole society will be prosperous. (D. Xie 1989, 2)[2]

The program was initially designed to remedy the social unrest and disorder presumed to have been created by economic development. Problems such as an increase in divorce and adolescent crimes, neglect of the elderly, and widespread youth behavior problems have become major concerns of the state. It was hoped that the Mothers' Workshops Program would help to pull family members together and restore traditional values in the local community (D. Xie 1989).

To accomplish these goals, the Mothers' Workshops Program promotes improvement in four areas: ethics and morality, sanitation and public health, homemaking and productive skills, and leisure activities and social services. Women in the local community are to be educated in ethics so that they will "practice proper etiquette, respect womanly virtues, pay attention to motherhood, and increase harmony in the family" (Zhao 1984, 25). Courses on homemaking, sanitation, interior decoration, and the art of makeup teach women such things as nutritious food preparation for family members, the proper makeup to wear when accompanying their husbands to social gatherings, and how to take care of the elderly with chronic diseases. Training in productive skills is connected with the "Living Rooms as Factories" program. Courses on leisure activities, planning, and social services encourage women to organize themselves "to visit the elderly, orphans, the handicapped, the mentally retarded, and families of military servicemen or families in poverty (in the local community)" in their leisure time (Zhao 1984, 26). Behind various activities of the Mothers' Workshops is a revised image of modern womanhood. As the person in charge of the training courses for supervisors of the Mothers' Workshops stated in an article, "In modern society, women have to play at least four different roles: they have to be pretty women, lovely wives, responsible mothers, and successful professionals/workers" (M. Xie 1985, 60).

Numerous Mothers' Workshops have been conducted with the KMT's encouragement and sponsorship. Beginning in 1977, the state organized regular training courses for supervisors who ran the Mothers' Workshops in local communities. The same year, the government published a ten-volume textbook called *Mama Duben* (Mothers' Readers) to guide and promote the Mothers Workshops Program (Taiwan Shengzhengfu Shehuichu 1977).

Additional materials followed.[3] By 1989 a total of 8,130 supervisors had been trained by the government and 160,000 copies of textbooks had been published and distributed. Every year the state collects statistics on the number of Mothers' Workshops actually held in the local community. Government officials also make regular trips to local communities to evaluate the program. Devoted local officials and supervisors are selected and honored.

The prevalence of the Mothers' Workshops program can be shown by the number of classes held in the local community. A nationwide survey conducted in 1982 indicates that, among the 1,526 randomly selected residents, 75 percent said that Mothers' Workshops had been organized in their communities,[4] and 51 percent of these communities held regular Mothers' Workshops classes. The survey found that 22 percent of the interviewees attended class regularly and 31 percent did so on ad hoc basis (Taiwan Shengzhengfu Yanjiu Kaohe Fazhan Weiyunhui 1983, 178–83). By 1984, 4,063 of a total of 4,324 communities in Taiwan had implemented the Community Development Program. In 1984, 89.3 percent of those communities organized a Mothers' Workshop as part of their Community Development Program. One-third of the counties and cities (seven out of a total of twenty-one) had a community sponsor rate of 90 percent. Among those seven counties and cities, three had a Mothers' Workshop in every local community (Zhao 1984, 26).[5]

The workshop sessions are usually held at community centers on the weekend. Classes such as sewing, cooking, flower arranging, snack

TABLE 2.1
Number of Classes and Attendance Rate of Mothers' Workshops at
Tainan County, Taiwan, 1985 and 1986

| Courses and Activities | Total Classes | | Attendance | | Attendance per Class | |
|---|---|---|---|---|---|---|
| | 1985 | 1986 | 1985 | 1986 | 1985 | 1986 |
| Family relations (mother and son, spouses, mother-in-law and daughter-in-law) | 100 | 35 | 1,342 | 976 | 13.4 | 27.9 |
| Public health (sanitation, family planning, emergency care) | 90 | 57 | 1,402 | 1,004 | 15.6 | 17.6 |
| Homemaking (cooking, flower arrangement, interior decoration) | 308 | 170 | 2,735 | 1,725 | 8.9 | 10.1 |
| New knowledge (crime prevention, makeup, social skills) | 84 | 79 | 1,628 | 1,234 | 19.4 | 15.6 |
| Productive skills (bamboo handicrafts, embroidery, knitting, toys, ornaments, pin making) | 66 | 61 | 851 | 612 | 12.9 | 10.0 |
| Recreation activities (camping, barbecue, folk dancing) | 707 | 659 | 3,522 | 4,126 | 5.0 | 6.3 |
| Social services (visiting the elderly and poor, community services) | 68 | 79 | 536 | 350 | 7.9 | 4.4 |
| Total | 1,423 | 1,140 | 12,016 | 10,027 | | |

SOURCE: Taiwansheng Mamajiaoshi Fudao Renyuan Yanxihui (1987, 32–33).

making, household decoration, social etiquette, the art of make up, folk
dancing, and family planning have been included in the Mothers' Workshops. Table 2.1 lists classes offered in local communities in Tainan
County in 1985 and 1986 (Taiwansheng Mamajiaoshi Fudao Renyuan
Yanxihui 1987, 32–33). It also shows the attendance over these two
years. More than one thousand classes with more than ten thousand participants were organized in Tainan County in both 1985 and 1986. Un-

fortunately, the figures do not show how many of the participants were frequent attenders. In other words, we do not know if there were more than ten thousand individuals participating in the Mothers Workshops Program, or if the ten thousand participants went to various classes and sessions over the years. However, the table does show that the most frequently sponsored courses are recreation oriented.[6] Women were particularly attracted to courses on makeup, family relationships, and public health.

The "Living Rooms as Factories" program, referred to as the "family subsidiary employment program," was designed to bring the surplus labor of communities and families into productive work. In the late 1960s and early 1970s, several surveys were conducted to measure the extent and nature of surplus labor in various communities. A project report, *How to Promote Family Subsidiary Work through the Community Development Program,* explained at length how mobilization in the local community would eventually lead to higher productivity at the national level.

> The goals of this project are to fully utilize manpower, to accelerate economic growth, to improve production methods, and to promote societal development. In terms of economic growth, this project will evaluate the level of surplus labor in the community, aiming at mobilizing the surplus labor into productive work. The purposes are to release the pressures of labor shortages in the factory, to slow down wage increases due to labor shortages, and to decrease the costs of production, such as investment in factory facilities and dormitories, and costs of management and recruitment, by using family subsidiary employment, and to promote new export products. The goals are fourfold: increasing productivity, decreasing costs, stabilizing consumer prices, and accelerating economic development (Xinzhengyuan 1978, 2).

The "Living Rooms at Factories" proposal was developed because these surveys found that there were many "idle women" in the community (Xingzhengyuan 1978, 2). The government provided special loans for families intending to purchase machines to do homework. Day-care centers were strategically established to free mothers from family responsibilities, but not to diminish their "mother" role. Workshops were conducted, and housewives were trained. Many families' living rooms were converted into "factories," housewives became workers, and work became domesticated. The 1982 nationwide survey indicates that, among the 1,526 randomly selected residents, 46 percent said that Living Rooms as Factories programs had been organized in their communities, and 38 percent of these communities held the classes regularly. Whenever the classes were held, 15 percent of the interviewees were regular attenders and 38 percent attended occasionally (Taiwan Sheng-zhengfu Yanjiu Kaohe Fazhan Weiyuanhui 1983, 178–82).

The impact of these programs on married women, unfortunately, is difficult to establish because no relevant statistics are available. However, self-reported figures gathered in 1982 from community residents do indicate that these programs were more than self-congratuating propagada on the KMT's part. Among those surveyed, two-thirds stated that the Living Rooms as Factories program helped to improve the welfare of their families. As for the Mothers' Workshops program, three-fourths of the respondents found that the program enhanced the quality of their family lives (Taiwan Shengzhengfu Yanjiu Kaohe Fazhan Weiyuanhui 1983, 183–85). Another indirect way to estimate the influence of the Living Rooms as Factories program is to compare its public assessment with that of the Family Planning Program, for which we do have relevant statistics to indicate its influence.[7] Survey data indicate that more than three-fourths of the interviewees believed that the family planning program had either made a "significant" or "noticeable" difference. The figures for the Living Rooms as Factories were 17 percent and 42 percent, respectively.[8] In geographical terms more than 50 percent of the interviewees from agricultural, fishing, and township communities said that the Living Rooms as Factories program had a significant or a noticeable impact. The figures range from 71 percent to 97 percent for the family planning program (Taiwan Shengzhengfu Yanjiu Kaohe Fazhan Weiyuanhui 1983, 189–201). These numbers suggest that the general public in Taiwan does respond to some, if not all, state-sponsored programs.

From a broader perspective, families whose female members did homework in their living rooms were not the only beneficiaries of these programs. Capitalists were relived of a labor shortage in the factories and spared potential upward pressure on wages. To the extent that living rooms were converted into "factories," the capitalists were able to spend less on factory facilities, energy, dormitories, and management. The society as a whole was able to benefit from productivity increases, consumer price stabilization, economic growth, and the reduction of conflict between capitalists and workers.

Through the Living Rooms as Factories program, the state has become an agent of capitalist production and accumulation. Its role is sometimes in direct conflict with women's interests; more generally, it fails to protect women against capitalist exploitation. For example, in the name of Living Rooms as Factories, one local official in a community became the contractor who pressured female homeworkers to work for the specific factories he represented. As a result, the community development office was in direct conflict with the female contractor and female homeworkers in the locality. The female contractor saw the local official as an intruder who tried to take some of "her workers" away from her. The female homeworkers felt coerced to give up their original piece rate for a lower one (Xinzhengyuan 1978).

In another incident, the community center was lent to the factory as a production site. Housewives in the neighborhood were gathered to work there. During my visit in the summer of 1989, local officials told female workers who were paid below the minimum wage to lie about their wages. One woman finally told me the truth, "They told us not to tell you our real wages. They said the wages are so low that it will make us look bad."

In some communities, local officials have generated revenue from the Living Rooms as Factories program. When I asked the manager of the same factory about the low wages the women received, he replied, "Every month, we take out a small amount of their wages and put it aside. The money is used for our donation to the office for the community development program. In any case, those women would not have been able to work if Mr. Chang (the local director) didn't let them use the community center."[9] In this case, when female homeworkers work, both the capitalist and the state benefit.

More generally, individual homeworkers make up the lowest level of the production workforce in Taiwan's satellite manufacturing system wherever subcontracting is prevalent. The importance of subcontracting production to factories that contract the work out is widely recognized among factory owners. As one owner told me, "Without subcontracting, given the current facilities of our factory, our total production would be cut down to only one-third." The statistical data collected by the government show that, in 1988, an average of 11.6 percent of the gross profit of the manufacturing industry was created by workers laboring under subcontracting arrangements (Jinjibu 1988, 6). Although the figure does not show how much of the work is contracted out to female homeworkers, as opposed to small factories, the idea that living rooms can, and to some extent should, be used for factory production, and that housewives can and should contribute to national economic development through homeworking, legitimizes a specific form of surplus value appropriation and capital accumulation.

Finally, and most important, the Mothers' Workshops and Living Rooms as Factories programs represent the KMT's effort to reconcile the potential conflict between female labor-force participation and women's role in the family. Through the Mothers' Workshops, the state reinforces traditional gender ideology. During the process of Taiwan's economic development, the KMT state has actively and purposefully advocated traditional ethics and virtues that emphasize women's moral obligation to their country. The traditional ideology encourages women to take on more responsibilities in a period of social change. Through the Living Rooms as Factories program, married women are incorporated into productive labor not as regular workers but as homeworkers, reinforcing their subordinate and dependent status in the family and society. Their labor-force participation is based on its subsidiary and supplementary character.

## Labor Law in Taiwan

The massive government campaign promoting the latest version of womanhood tells only half the story about the patriarchal nature of Taiwan's satellite factory system. The specific power relations between owners and workers are defined by the labor laws promulgated by the government. Before 1984 labor relations in Taiwan were governed by the Union Law of 1929 and the Factory Law of 1931. Although these outdated laws no longer applied to the situation in Taiwan, revision did not truly get under way until several disasters in the late 1960s aroused public opinion. Even after that, it took another ten years to get the current Standard Labor Law established. Throughout the years, several versions of the new law were turned down by the Legislative Yuan either because of protest from the capitalists or because of concern about the law's effects on the economic climate. Since passage of the Standard Labor Law in 1984, controversy has focused, in particular, on issues of retirement, overtime, and overtime pay, layoffs, and protection for female labor. I shall limit my discussion to overtime and to wages, both regular and overtime.

According to the Standard Labor Law, workers can be asked to work up to eight hours a day and no more than forty-eight hours a week. For every six days, the workers should get at least one day off as *lijia,* that is, routine break. Every year, the workers also get *xiujia,* or vacation time.

During both their *lijia* and *xiujia* the workers are entitled to their regular wages. Part of the vacation time is fixed; that is, in Taiwan, there is a total of sixteen official holidays each year. The remainder of each worker's vacation time is decided by the number of years he/she has worked for the current employer. For example, a worker will be granted a seven-day vacation each year after he/she has worked for the current employer for more than one year but less than three years. The number of days goes up as the number of years worked for the same employer increases, to an upper limit of thirty days a year.

Only under special circumstances, such as seasonal fluctuations or unpredictable natural disasters, can the owners ask workers to work overtime. According to the 1984 law, the overtime should not exceed three hours per day for male workers and two hours for female workers. The total number of overtime hours per month should be no more than forty-six hours for males and twenty-four hours for females. Only in industries specified by the central government can overtime be as high as four hours per day to a total of forty-six hours for males and thirty-two hours for females per month; however, no list of specified industries is provided.

When overtime is requested under special circumstances, the employers have to receive either the union's or the workers' consent. They are also required to notify, and get approval from, the local official before any decision is carried out. The law reminds the employers to "compensate the workers with appropriate time to recuperate" (Laogong Xingzheng Zazhishe 1989, 10–11). The "appropriate time" is later defined as "at least a total of twelve hours between the time when the workers stop working and the time they restart work" (Laogong Xingzheng Zazhishe 1989, 171–72).

With regard to workers' earnings, the law states that the wage rate should be decided by the employer and employee, but the total amount of a worker's earnings should not be lower than the standard wage announced by the central government every year.[10] Payment for overtime varies according to the number of hours the workers are asked to work. When overtime is less than two hours, the workers receive a 33.3 percent increase in the hourly rate. The increase reaches 66.6 percent when the workers are asked to work more than two hours but less than four hours. If workers are asked to work during the routine break and vacation time, they are entitled to double wages.

From the written guidelines, it seems that the workers' welfare is well protected. In reality, this has not been the case. Most of the Standard Labor Law's regulations on overtime and overtime payment are regularly violated. The extent of such violations is especially severe in the satellite factories (see Chapter 5).

The political discourse that perpetuates such violations deserves analysis. The underlying political agenda of the Standard Labor Law is stated in the first amendment to the law: "to protect the workers' rights and welfare, to reinforce a cooperative relationship between the workers and capitalists, and to promote societal and economic development." This basic agenda has produced numerous instances where the workers' welfare is compromised for the sake of capitalist interests and of Taiwan's economic development. For example, when calculating the standard wage, the state has adopted a formula designed to "take the capitalist's burden into consideration" (San 1988, 24). There are two components in the formula: (1) the necessary value that an employed worker has to earn in order to meet the basic current living standard,[11] and (2) the actual average monthly earnings of an employed person calculated across the entire manufacturing sector. According to the same report, the second component was included specifically to "bring down the level of standard wages" and, therefore, to relieve the pressures that would otherwise be felt among the capitalists (San 1988, 24). Without including the second component, the standard wage level of 1988 would have been NT$8,654 per month instead of NT$8,130 (San 1988, 22–25).

Besides, when the law states that the *earnings* of the workers should not be lower than the level of the standard wage set by the state, it actually compares two figures with different components. As stated in the Law, *earnings* are defined as workers' "regular income," including both earnings during regular working hours and overtime; the standard wage, however, counts workers' earning during regular working hours only. By definition, therefore, it is almost impossible for a worker's *earnings* to be lower than the standard wage. Nevertheless, in 1987 more than 15 percent of workers in manufacturing earned less than the standard wage level announced by the central government. That is, even after including their overtime payments, a significant number of workers were still paid below the legal standard set by the state. In 1988 about 60 percent of the workers who earned less than the standard wages were in manufacturing. Of female workers who earned less than the standard wages, about two-thirds were manufacturing; and in the manufacturing sector, more than one-fifth of female workers earned less than the standard wage (DGBAS 1988, Table 31, p. 90).

The state not only has adopted a passive role in enforcing the Standard Labor Law, but has also actively suppressed whatever attempts workers have made to challenge capitalist exploitation. For three decades, under martial law, strikes and protests were declared illegal. Although martial law was lifted in 1987, the state still exerts strong control over routine union activities. For example, a local official in the Office of Industrial Relations told me in an interview that the staff of a union has to be approved by government officials. The union also needs to get official approval before it can hold a meeting. The union is required to report its decisions at meetings to local officials. If the officials denounce any of the decisions as illegal, those decisions have to be abandoned. Whenever there has been a conflict between the workers and the owners, the state has allied itself with the owners. It either used police force to harass the protesters and union leaders or reinterpreted the bylaws in such a way that the workers lost their legal right to go on stroke. In 1989 the first strike in Taiwan's history ended unsuccessfully. The union leader May-wen Lo was fired in the middle of a union drive. The subsequent strike was later declared illegal, and May-wen Lo was charged with illegal conduct. During the struggle, May-wen Lo, in turn, challenged the legality of the employer's decision in firing him based on the Union Law, Title 37, which states that "in the period of capitalist-worker confrontation, the employers cannot fire the workers because they participate in capitalist-worker confrontation" (Wu, n.d., 255). He eventually lost the case. The Supreme Court decided that, in the process of mobilizing the workers to go on strike, May-wen Lo "had jeopardized the employer's reputation and therefore disrupted the ethics surrounding the employer-employee relationship. The activities he organized also violated the employees' obligation to show loyalty and respect to their employer" (*Shijie Ribao* 1990). Therefore, the Supreme Court declared that the employer's decision to fire May-wen Lo was lawful and that the strike was illegal because it was organized by him after he had been fired. May-wen Lo was sentenced to two years in prison.

## The Creation of Harmonious Labor Relations

Workers' struggles against oppressive labor practices are curtailed by the procapitalist and pro–economic growth political discourse fostered by the state. This ideology is most evident in the educational programs sponsored by the state to create harmonious labor relations and in situations where the state is called upon to mediate in labor disputes. The Supreme Court's decision in the May-wen Lo case accurately reflects the principles used by the state in governing labor relations and resolving labor conflict. To understand the KMT's efforts to create harmonious labor relations in the late 1980s, it is useful to analyze the handbooks for workers' education published by the Labor Committee of the Executive Council after the lifting of martial law in 1987. *Labor Policy*, the first of sixteen handbooks in the series Materials for Workers' Education, lays out the goals, principles, and strategies of the state in dealing with "labor problems." It states that, under the guidance of the Three Principles, the state "gives priority to the national interest over class interest" (Laogong Xingzheng Zazhishe 1990a, 37). It emphasizes that

> although resolving issues concerning laborers is the purpose of our labor policy, its ultimate goal is to develop the national economy and promote societal welfare. . . . Therefore, the labor policy should be seen as part of the state's overall policy, instead of a separate entity in itself. It should be incorporated into our national policy accordingly. . . . When formulating its labor policy or making decisions on other related issues, the state has to work within the premise of sound socioeconomic development. It cannot treat it simply as a matter of the interest of one particular class. (Laogong Xingzheng Zazhishe 1990a, 3).

In another handbook, *The Ethics of Relations between Workers and Capitalists*, Taiwan's economic development is attributed to the harmonious relationship between the workers and capitalists over the last three decades. Disputes between workers and capitalists in the late 1980s are interpreted as a breakdown of traditional moral norms:

> Our economic progress in the last three decades had been based entirely on a harmonious laborer-capitalist relationship. As the result of our economic development, . . . there have been dramatic changes in the ways people relate to one another. Now, as the new moral norms are yet to be established, there is a huge gap between the level of our economic achievement and people's moral standards. This is manifested by the fact that we have had so many disputes between employers and workers in recent years, especially after the passage of the Standard Labor Law in 1984. (Laogong Xingzheng Zazhishe 1990b, 1)

In order to restore a harmonious relationship, the handbook calls for the creation of a new set of moral norms between the employers and workers. The moral norms are defined as behavior codes applicable to employers and workers in dealing with one another. The handbook lays out the norms in terms of relative and absolute obligations:

> When we talk about the worker-capitalist relationship, there is a unique aspect to it. That is, there are two components in the relationship: the relative obligation and absolute obligation. The relative obligation means that one need not fulfill his obligation if the other party fails to realize his. The absolute obligation means that one is not exempted from his obligation even when the other party fails his/hers. In other words, no matter how rude or harsh the other becomes, based on the moral standards applicable to all human beings, you should still carry out whatever obligation you are supposed to carry out. The absolute obligation between the workers and capitalists is the essence of what we call the moral norms between the workers and capitalists. (Laogong Xingzheng Zazhishe 1990b, 10)

The handbook further elaborates the ethics with which workers should comply. For example, based on "the principles of fairness and loyalty," the worker should not take a side job without the employer's permission because "due to overwork and exhaustion, this (taking a side job) will lower the (worker's) productive quality and hence jeopardize the employer's interest." In other words, it is morally wrong if the workers do not "make themselves available, in the best possible condition, to their employer" (Laogong Xingzheng Zazhishe 1990b, 12). Drinking and other improper habits after work are discouraged for the same reason. "As decent human beings," the handbook states, the workers should maximize their own productivity on the shop floor to "create increasing profits for the employers" (Laogong Xingzheng Zazhishe 1990b, 13). Getting into the same line of business as their employer, either during or after their period of employment, is seen as an immoral act because this could "create furious competition between oneself and one's employer and therefore bring one's loyalty and trust into question" (Laogong Xingzheng Zazhishe 1990b, 18).

In contrast, the moral norms enjoyed by the employers are mostly in the domain of "relative obligation" so that, according to the definition, they need only be carried out when the other party complies. Or they apply where the workers in any case enjoy certain entitlements under the current law. For example, the employers are reminded to pay their workers on time and in currency,[12] not to put their workers in hazardous working conditions, and to have their workers insured (Laogong Xingzheng Zazhishe 1990b, 20–28).

In dealing with the increasing tension between workers and employers and the confrontational style of worker protest, the Labor Committee calls for "an aggressive promotion of worker-capitalist cooperation, paying attention to the interest of the workers and capitalists, and putting effort into economic development" (Laogong Xingzheng Zazhishe 1990c, 19). To achieve these goals, it identifies strategies in two categories: (1) to reduce disputes by clarifying the contract and promoting regular meetings of workers and capitalists; and (2) to enhance harmonious relations by advocating the ideal of "factory as family, factory as school," promoting a movement to "increase productivity," establishing a cooperative ideological consciousness, and publicly praising factories with good worker-capitalist relationships (meaning with no disputes occurring) (Laogong Xingzheng Zazhishe 1990c, 19).

These strategies show that the state places an absolute value on Taiwan's economic development. Other issues that are, or may potentially be, in conflict with this ultimate goal have to be suppressed. Class conflict is considered to be one such issue. The construction of harmonious labor relations underlies the state's labor policy. Within it the workers are not conceptualized as a class who should get, or bargain for, fair treatment when they sell their labor. Instead, they are coached to follow workers' ethics even under exploitative circumstances. To practice the moral norms daily, the workers are also encouraged to be superproductive. In dealing with the rise of working-class consciousness and the increase in labor disputes of the late 1980s, the state set out a countercampaign that encouraged cooperation and discouraged confrontation.

For workers in the satellite factories, the protective strength of the Standard Labor Law is very limited. First, according to the law, only factories with more than thirty workers are required to make public in writing their regulations on such matters as overtime, wages, promotions, routine breaks, vacation time, and the handling of disputes (Laogong Xingzheng Zazhishe 1989, 20–21). Without written regulations, owners of the satellite factories enjoy more leverage and fewer constraints in organizing the workplace. Second, under regulations specified by the Union Law, only in factories with more than thirty workers can the workers organize a union.[13] Workers in the satellite factories are thus deprived of the right to defend themselves collectively. The individual worker is left to strive for personal survival. For workers in the satellite factories, expecting the law or union to protect them from oppressive labor practices has been, and continues to be, unrealistic. Besides, individual workers need to now exactly to what protection and rights they are entitled, before they can take any possible action to defend their rights.

## "The People Rule, Not the Law"

In the prevailing political environment in Taiwan, owners of satellite factories enjoy the freedom to operate their factories as they see fit. One manager stated proudly that, in Chinese society, "it is the people who rule, not the law." According to him, "In other countries, they rely on a set of regulations. Here, regulations are only secondary. It's the people who are in charge. We Chinese rely on connections and people, not that much on regulations or law."

Another manager told me how it was possible to use the norms and behavior patterns of Chinese society to the capitalists' advantage:

> We managers are the mediators between the boss and the workers. We have to communicate their [the workers'] opinion to the boss, while at the same time watching out for the boss's pocket. . . . It isn't really a bad thing if the workers are not happy with their wages. It implies that they have the potential to be worth more. How to manipulate them all depends on us, the managers. . . . Chinese are humble. We seldom talk about how good we are, not to mention boast. When things come down to wage conflicts, I always turn the issue around by asking the workers to give me a figure. That is, I ask them to tell me exactly how much more they believe their labor is worth. If they can't come out with a concrete price, then, they have to listen to me. I may decide to give them a raise. I may not. It's all up to me. Even if they do give me a price, the chances are it will always be lower than the real value of their labor. For example, if what they really want is a one-hundred-dollar raise, as Chinese they will only say that their labor is worth eighty dollars more, at the most. When this happens, I can easily cut it to fifty dollars. . . . By handling it this way, their productivity will go up because I do show them that I did recognize their unrest [and give them a raise]. . . . It is a win–win battle for the company when things come down to wage conflict, you know.

This manager believes that his way of handling the wage conflict has won the workers' hearts because the workers see him as on their side. Whenever excessive demands are placed on the workers, the workers tend to accept the imposition because they feel they are doing a personal favor to the manager to pay him back for what he has done for them.

The sense of fairness that workers develop in the satellite factories is largely shaped by what they perceive as possible or realistic. Regarding wages, workers see themselves as people earning a living through *xuehanqian* (blood and sweat money). Working overtime is usually presented by the employer as a chance for the workers to earn extra money. The pay some of them receive for their routine Sunday break is perceived as "free money" and, therefore, a favor provided through the employer's kindness. The variation in treatment among the factories or within each factory is thus attributed to the owner's personality. For example, some factories provide free meals. Others have a three-hour evening shift, rather than three and a half hours. Still others give the workers two-hundred-dollar bonuses for the spring festival. The workers' typical response to such benefits is "That owner is a nicer person."

## Conclusions

The relationship between the state and petty capitalist mode of production in the twentieth century is quite different from Hill Gates' finding for the premodern period in China. This chapter illustrates two important ways in which the state has intervened in the course of Taiwan's economic development. Government policies have helped to define women's productive and reproductive responsibilities and have played a major role in structuring the relations between workers and capitalists. Within the satellite factory system, programs such as Living Rooms as Factories and Mothers' Workshops influence both the political and ideological discourse. The capitalists, encouraged by the prodevelopment and procapitalist orientation of the state, have taken the law relating to labor control into their own hands. The state, concurrently, amounts to a beneficial recipient of the patriarchal system and capitalist development. Overall, state programs and policies establish the tone of labor relations and set the limits within which labor politics and workers' resistance are played out on the shop floor.

# 3 The Satellite Factory System from Within

When I first enquired about Taiwan's satellite factories, people told me what they had seen or experienced.

> There was a factory in the next building. They made caps for Kung-nan [a large sportswear factory in Taiwan]. My next-door neighbor used to sew logos on the caps. Her living room was really a mess. Every time I visited her, she was on the machine.
>
> . . . [Have you ever thought about doing it too?]
>
> Yes, I did. But my kid was too small. At that time, my sister's office mate was looking for someone to baby-sit her newborn baby. I ended up baby-sitting for her.
>
> You mean women do factory work at home?
>
> Oh, yeah. Many housewives do that as a subsidiary job. I have seen that. In fact, my brother's wife used to put together tiny Santa Clauses [Christmas ornaments] at home. I don't remember exactly how much she earned. Not that much, as I recall. When I visited her, I sometimes helped her. . . . No, it's not that complicated. All you do is to . . .

Even though piles of half-sewn caps in someone's corridor, living room, or backyard have become a common scene in many local communities in Taiwan, I was often amazed by the number of factories in the middle of rice fields, of workshops on the second or third floor of apartment buildings, and of homeworkers tending their small children, buying vegetables when the peddler comes by, and simultaneously packaging screws for the factory. Because most factories don't put up signs, and some do not even have a name, people usually relied upon locally recognized landmarks to give me directions. On my scooter, after getting lost, asking around, and having some luck, I would eventually be able to find the factory by following a direction such as this one:

> Go straight for about ten minutes. When you see a patch of taro on the right, make a left turn. Not far away from there, you'll see a *Thotekong* [the god of the land/earth] shrine underneath a banyan tree. It's right there. You can't miss it. Make a right turn. You'll then go across a bridge, see a patch of green beans, green onions, and bitter melons on your left and rice fields on your right, and pass a small stand selling cold drinks, incense, and cigarettes. Take the road next to the stand. Go across the railroad track. After about another five minutes, you will see two farmhouses. The one on the right, with a shack in the front yard, is Mr. Chang's factory. If you have difficulty finding it, ask the woman selling cold drinks. She'll tell you.

Taiwanese like to talk about stories of *baishou chengjia,* going from rags to riches. Many people believe that the growth of the satellite factories has created upward mobility for those who are willing to work hard. Observers say that the Chinese in Taiwan have the "boss syndrome": all want to be their own boss (Chang 1988). A local joke goes, "Throw a rock out of a window and the odds are good for hitting the general manager or president of a Taiwanese company."

The following sections address issues of the structural constraints embedded in Taiwan's export-led economy, the prospects of upward mobility thus created for men and women, and the internal and external organization of the satellite factory system. My discussion is intended to answer the following questions: How is the cost of uncertainty and fluctuation that trickles down from the global market absorbed, and by whom? What are the chances of success for individuals who aspire to become their own boss? What types of opportunities for upward mobility have been presented to working-class men and women over the last decades? And, what are the implications of the satellite factory system for Taiwan's overall class and gender stratification?

## Taiwan's Export-led Economy and the Satellite Factory System

Researchers have referred to Taiwan's relationship with the world economy as "dependent development," "marketing dependency," or "international subcontracting" (Griffen 1973; Amsden 1979; Barret and

Whyte 1982; Greenhalgh 1988). Although it is beyond the scope of this book to discuss each aspect fully, two general characteristics of Taiwan's export-led economy are relevant to my discussion of the satellite factory system. The first concerns types of products and their production. Ever since Taiwan shifted its economic orientation from import substitution to export manufacturing in the 1960s, its export industry has been concentrated on the production of light, low-value-added, consumer goods. Products such as shoes, garments, umbrellas, and electronic appliances are made by unskilled labor through an intensive and divisible production process. Access to cheap and disciplined labor is therefore vital to Taiwan's competitiveness in the international market.

The second unique feature of Taiwan's export-led economy has to do with a highly specialized division of labor among local manufacturers, trading companies, and international buyers. In his recent study of Taiwan's shoe industry, Skoggard roughly identifies three distinctive phases along an international commodity production chain that connects local producers with foreign markets: production, trading/exporting, and marketing (Skoggard 1993). The highly specialized division of labor along the chain means that Taiwanese manufacturers rarely have direct contact with foreign buyers, nor independent access to international markets. The choice of models or styles they produce and how much is produced are mainly determined by orders received from trading companies, whereas marketing in foreign countries is entirely in the hands of international buyers.

One of the detrimental effects of these two features on factories involved in manufacturing for export is that there is no long-term relationship among local producers, trading companies, and international buyers. While international buyers are constantly searching around the globe for comparable products made by the cheapest available labor, trading companies form only fragile bonds with local producers. This fragile partnership gives few incentives to local manufacturers, who have no direct involvement in marketing, to invest in research and development in order to create their own brands. Switching into a new line of production, or imitating a specific product after one factory makes a profit with it, is therefore common practice in Taiwan (Myers 1986, 55). Competition at the international level is thus translated into cutthroat competition among local producers. As the manager of one trading company explained to me,

The competition here is fierce and sometimes brutal. For some orders, factories are willing to cut the prices to a level that is even lower than the cost. They hope to compensate for this with other orders they might get [contingently] where the profit is good. Foreign buyers have been spoiled in Taiwan. They are more than happy to go along with the competition. We, the trading companies, sometimes really have mixed feelings about the whole issue of price-cutting competition.

Factories producing for export thus exist in a highly unstable and competitive marketplace, in which "numerous enterprises emerge and fail every day" (Myers 1986, 55). Government records show that a factory established in 1981 had little more than a two-thirds chance of surviving into 1986. And among the approximately 119,000 factories operating in 1986, fewer than half had been established within the last five years. The survival rate was especially low among small-scale and labor-intensive factories (DGBAS 1988, 17–18). Between 1981 and 1986, the establishments with the lowest survival rates were leather-goods factories (45.3 percent) and garment factories (54.0 percent); chemical products (89.2 percent) and precision instruments (99.0 percent) had the highest rates of survival (see DGBAS 1988, Table 2.1). Research expenditure did not exceed 10 percent in any the listed industries, but those with a low survival rate spent a lot less on research.

These data indicate that although the international market may have provided opportunities for the growth of local factories, any given entrepreneur's (or establishment's) chances of success are dim. Workers who strive to escape from their proletarian status by starting small factories therefore encounter a low success rate. Even those that do make it seldom move beyond petty bourgeois status. Furthermore, the high mortality rate among small-scale and labor-intensive factories produces a highly unstable labor market. Workers who take advantage of the employment opportunities in export-oriented enterprises frequently face the shutdown of their factory. Between 1986 and 1988 the proportion of involuntary job losses that resulted from factory shutdowns fell from three-quarters to two-thirds. Meanwhile, however, the percentage of job losses that occurred when a "seasonal or temporary job [was] completed" increased significantly, from less than one-fifth in 1986 to more than a quarter in 1988 (see DGBAS 1988, Table 2.2).[1] In this period, the manufacturing sector contributed between 40 percent and 70 percent of involuntary job losses, much more than any other sector.

For women, the effect of low factory survival rates and high involuntary job loss is twofold. First, female workers as a group are disadvantaged because women tend to be concentrated in labor-intensive factories, which have the lowest survival rate. Second, married female workers face special difficulties. Women whose husbands run a family factory can encounter situations that impose specific difficulties. They must either devote themselves to the family business so that it might have a better chance of survival or face the consequences of possible shutdowns, including the need to look for jobs in factories belonging to others. Women whose husbands do not own a factory are in an even worse position. They have to bear the burden of frequent job changes with no prospect of accumulating seniority. Before I further discuss married women's experiences in the satellite factory system, it is necessary to examine that system more closely.

## The Organizational Structure of the Satellite Factory System

The satellite factory system, which is such a notable feature of Taiwan's export-led economy, can be analyzed in relation to two interconnected questions: How does the system mobilize local financial and human resources for international production? And how are the costs and risks of export manufacturing distributed among individual producers? Focusing on these questions will allow me to explore in greater detail how the satellite factory system functions to enhance Taiwan's relative competitiveness in the global market.

At the organizational level, the satellite factory system links a large number of small-scale factories specialized in various aspects of production through subcontracting networks. For example, six basic types of factory can be identified in the process of producing wooden jewelry boxes: box body factory, painting factory, flannel factory, glass factory, hardware factory, and assembly factory. In the box body factory, the wooden boards are cut, carved, and then assembled into drawers, doors/lids, and wooden boxes according to a sample. These wooden boxes, referred to as "raw bodies," are then sent to the painting factory for painting and polishing. The glass factory produces sculptural, stained, or frosted glass to decorate the doors of the wooden jewelry boxes. The hardware factory supplies all kinds of metal parts—for example, handles, hinges, screws, and hangers—to the assembly factory. In the assembly factory, the different parts of the wooden jewelry box are put together.

The tasks include sticking in the drawers, screwing on the handles, affixing the glass to the doors, attaching the doors to the boxes, and inspecting the music device when a wooden jewelry box is turned into a music box. After all these steps, the boxes are wrapped and packed for shipping.

The satellite factory system thus is organized to absorb structural constraints embedded in Taiwan's export-led growth. Production costs and business risks that would have been borne by the owner of a large factory are now shared by, and diversified among, a large number of individual entrepreneurs who are linked together in a pyramid-shaped network consisting of "center" and "satellite" factories. The factory's profit margin, and hence chances of survival, decrease as one moves from the "center" to the "satellite" or from the upper to the lower levels of the pyramid. Let me demonstrate why this is so by first discussing the relational position between "center" and "satellite" factories.

In actual fact, any one factory can be both a center and a satellite. Thus the assembly factory in the example of wooden jewelry box production is clearly the center factory, and the other five types of factories are its satellites. Yet a box body factory can itself be considered a center factory if it subcontracts the drawers, doors, or even the front part of the drawers to other specialized factories. The same is true for the hardware factory, which may sell metal parts to the assembly factory, but only make one or two of the metal parts itself. The rest of its merchandise may come from nearby small workshops where only hinges, handles, or screws are produced.

A factory at the top and "center" is more profitable than the "satellite" one at the bottom. This is true not only because each subcontracting transaction involves surplus value appropriation from the producer (satellite) to the contractor (center), but also because a factory may forge a center-satellite relationship by selling overflow orders to other factories in the same line of production for a commission. Such a relationship is often initiated by factories on the upper levels of the pyramid, since there is enough profit margin to be further divided. During my fieldwork observation a number of assembly factories revealed to me that they have made easy profits by getting more work orders from the trading company than their factories could actually fill and then selling the excess work orders to other assembly factories. Looking at the satellite factory system as a whole, it becomes clear that production costs and business risks are borne unevenly. Those at the top or "center" are in a much better position to reap the profit from, and pass along the cost to, their "satellite" factories. Last, and most important, a significant portion of their profits derives from their utilization of surplus labor.

Because Taiwan's export manufacturers concentrate their production on light, labor-intensive consumer goods, their competitive edge in the global market depends on the availability of cheap and disciplined labor. The satellite factory system, as an institution, allows producers to strengthen labor control, maximize labor productivity, and heighten the scope of labor mobilization in local communities. According to the factory owners, increases in labor control and high productivity result from the fact that numerous self-employed owners "voluntarily push themselves to the maximum," and "you've got a boss for every three to five workers." Factory owners of the "center" especially praise the subcontracting function of the system because it helps them to connect to workshops and to "discover" homeworkers in the local neighborhood. As one owner puts it, "Without them [the satellite factories and homeworkers], we would have no chance to make it." In fact, the owner of an assembly factory once told me that, in the satellite factory system, "small is beautiful." With pride, he stated,

> As an owner, I have other things to do. It's impossible for me to keep an eye on every worker in my own factory all day long. [With the subcontracting system] you get a boss for every two or three workers. Of course my productivity would be high. I have so many bosses in different factories working for me [to monitor the workers]. . . . This is like I have a hundred-some workers working for me. The only difference is that they are either their own bosses or they work for their immediate bosses. . . . People call my factory *big* not because I have twenty some workers. It is because, in the peak season, I can manage to produce twenty thousand pieces of jewelry boxes every month by using others' labor.

In order to "use others' labor" for their own purposes, factory owners need to maintain reasonably friendly relationships with others in the system. However, such interdependency simultaneously coexists with fierce competition among factories at various levels. On one level is the conflict and cooperation among factories of the same type. For example, the assembly factories compete with one another on price, number of work orders, and quantity of each work order when they do business with the trading company. There is also fierce competition among them when they contract work out to the box body, painting, and other factories. However, each factory is compelled to maintain good relationships with the other factories in the same category, so as to enhance its chances of receiving overflow work orders from them or of selling its own excess work orders to them at a good price.

Factories of different types exhibit a somewhat different variety of conflict and cooperation. For example, in order to make a higher profit, the assembly factory may seek to cut what it pays for parts to the lowest possible level when it contracts work out to the box body factory. However, if that price is too low, the box body factory may decide to turn down the unprofitable work order, or even to go out of business. As the owner of an assembly factory puts it, "Of course we want to cut the price. But we need to make sure there are enough box body factories around to choose from as well." Moreover, although an assembly factory is compelled to give its order to the box body factory that is willing to take the lowest price, a box body factory with a stable workforce and reasonable price is usually sought out by more than one assembly factory. Thus it takes more than money to get the box body factory to agree to squeeze more work orders into its already tight schedule.

As a result, factory owners make endless efforts to maneuver between competition and cooperation. The skills and practices of granting or requesting favors and saving face, on the one hand, and cultivating connections, on the other, are crucial to success. Quite often, skills and practices originally used to gain access to others' labor are deployed to attain scarce resources or in business negotiations. I first learned about the subtlety of business connections from A-tong, a driver and deliverer for an assembly factory. That day he needed to purchase several hundred pieces of a special type of wooden board from a factory. He informed me that we first had to pick up the owner of a box body factory, who would accompany us. When I asked him why, he replied,

> We have never done business with this raw material factory. All we need is several hundred pieces. The factory may think it's not a big enough order. Mr. Wang has done business with this factory for a long time. He has promised to help. Besides, the factory is in a small alley. It could be hard to find.

As another owner put it,

> We Chinese rely on connections. For example, when I need to buy some raw materials, I will get them from people I know. If they don't know you, sometimes they won't sell it to you. Not even if you are

willing to pay more. I mean, a product may be sold for ten dollars. If you don't know the person, you won't get it even if you are willing to pay eleven dollars. It all depends on connections. The Chinese are different from the Americans.

In a price-bargaining situation, playing meticulously with "saving face" can usually hasten the amicable closing of a deal. The bookkeeper in an assembly factory described this process in the case of contracting work out to its satellite factories:

> When I contact those satellite factories, I give them a price. This is what we call the initial price. [I asked her to explain that further.] The initial price is a price that I have to stick with. I won't agree to cut it no matter what they say. I leave the price bargaining part to Mr. Li [the owner]. . . . It won't work if Mr. Li offers the initial price himself and gets into the bargaining right away. Because [if we do that,] after a while others will think Mr. Li is not trustworthy. That's why it is usually me, a bookkeeper, giving out the initial price. Mr. Li can later tell others either "She doesn't know that much," "We are helping each other save face," or "It's because of you that I give you a cut." . . . In most of the cases, I can give out the price that Mr. Li eventually settles with. But, such a price has to come from the owner. It makes the whole business much easier.

There are other routines that ensure good relationships. Visiting one's satellite factories to cultivate relations is as important as checking on schedule and quality. After the initial greeting, it is customary to offer a cigarette, betel nut,[2] or a cold drink in the summer. One assembly factory owner explained why the gesture is important, "In a sense I am their boss. I give them work to do. But you can't calculate the relationship merely in terms of money. When I need them to rush my work for the deadlines, I owe them a favor." In exchange, the owner of a box body factory may host a feast in a restaurant when representatives from the trading company arrive to visit. After several drinks, the latter may ask the owner of the assembly factory to tighten up his quality control, while the owner of the boxy body factory may hint that he might have to turn down the next order if the price stays low. It is very likely that the feast will conclude with reassurances from everyone involved in the business that cooperation is the only way to survive under the current circumstances.

When describing the organization of the satellite factory system, it is important also to consider the makeup of the workforce. It consists of three types of workers: outsiders, insiders, and homeworkers. Both outsiders and insiders are wage workers who are paid at an hourly rate, even though most are hired on a daily basis. Homeworkers, on the other hand, are paid on a piece-rate basis. Physically, both outsiders and insiders carry out their work in the factory; the only difference is that outsiders are hired by a subcontractor who contracts work from the factory owner. The work of the factory usually involves special tasks that can be calculated easily on a piece-rate basis. For example, in Ta-you, an assembly factory, two groups of outsiders work on the shop floor fairly regularly alongside insiders. One group's work involves gluing the interior flannel into the boxes, while the other is responsible for screwing the hangers, doors, or handles on to the boxes. For the first group, the piece rate is calculated according to the size of the box and the complexity of the work involved. For the second group, the piece rate depends on how many screws and steps are involved. For a box with twenty screws, the price in 1989 was NT$4 (15 to 16 cents U.S.) apiece, with 20 cents per screw.[3]

Among these three groups, the outsiders receive the highest wages. For example, the average daily wage for female insiders is between NT$250 and NT$300, while the female outsiders usually get from NT$350 to NT$400 per day. Homeworkers can make around NT$320 per day if the factory gives them enough work. Workers often explain these discrepancies by saying that the outsiders' wages are higher than the homeworkers' because the former go to the factory to perform their task, while the factory has to deliver the work to the houses of the latter. Another "reason" given is that outsiders, unlike insiders, do not receive health insurance coverage. Of course, the outsiders can purchase health insurance by joining the occupational union, but they seldom do so. When asked, a woman replied, "When you work, you don't have time to get sick." The workers' perception is that the only function of the occupational union is to make health insurance available to self-employed workers or to those whose employers refuse to buy insurance for their workers.

The factory owners prefer to employ outsiders and homeworkers because, as one owner put it, "they're dynamic, fast, and flexible." According to him, "The work may take a whole week for the inside workers to finish. With the contracting workers, we need only five of them and they can get it done within three days." Another owner gave me a more detailed comparison.

> For example, if the pay rate is three hundred dollars per day for
> workers who work for us in the factory, we pay a rate equivalent to

four hundred and fifty dollars when we contract the work out. In other words, we pay fifty percent more to the workers who work for us through the putting-out system. This doesn't mean that it is more costly with the putting-out system. Because, for example, the amount of work that needs one hundred inside workers can easily be finished by forty outside workers, using the same amount of time. With the pay scale I mentioned, three hundred for insiders and four hundred and fifty for outsiders, we actually pay less for the same productivity level.

In addition, factory owners use contract workers to cope with the fluctuation of demand during the peak season and with the lack of work orders in the slack season. Especially during the slack season, the putting-out system decreases the owners' costs by minimizing factory expenses on overhead, factory facilities, and utilities such as fuel and light. As one owner put it:

> During the slack season, there isn't enough work. [With the putting-out system] I don't need to be responsible for the unnecessary workers. Besides, I would have spent more on managerial expenses, machines, and other facilities if there wasn't such a putting-out system.

Outsiders and homeworkers also merit higher wages than factory workers because, in terms of quality control and rejection rate, they produce a much higher return per worker than the insiders. Replying to my question as to how he exercised quality control with the contracting workers, a manager said that quality control is in fact incorporated into the piece-rate wage system. When insiders are asked to redo rejected items, it slows down the production process and consequently lowers the overall productivity of the factory. The homeworkers and outsiders have to redo rejected items at their own expense. Therefore,

> there is no problem with regard to quality control. It runs like a self-regulating mechanism. When they [the homeworkers] first start working for us, we exert tight control. The reject rate goes as high as thirty percent in the first month. From then on, we do not need to worry about the quality control anymore. The reject rate drops to zero after the second month. The reject rate in the factory always runs at an average level of twenty percent. The putting-out system has its own self-regulating mechanism as far as quality control is concerned.

In other words, in order to avoid having items rejected, the outsiders and homeworkers manage to produce goods more quickly and at a higher standard of quality. As a result, the owners actually receive a higher return from the putting-out system than from the inside system. By combining a minimum number of insiders with outsiders and homeworkers, the owners enjoy a maximum level of flexibility and stability in their labor supply. Another consequence is to weaken the employment, income, and job security of the insiders and so to enable the owner to substitute lower-cost labor.

As is to be expected, the division between insiders and outsiders has polarized workers in the satellite factory system. I learned about the tension between these two groups by unintentionally "crossing the line" in Cheng's box body factory. Three days after I started working there, Cheng introduced me to a group of outsiders who had come in to assemble the drawers. The work involved gluing five pieces of wooden board together into a drawer, holding it with a rubber band, putting the drawer aside to let it dry, and taking the rubber band off after the glue has dried and the drawer is in shape. After the initial introduction, I chatted with the outsiders as I worked with them. The next day, Ms. Chang, an insider in Cheng's factory, told me during the lunch break that there is a real difference between her work and the work of those "outsiders."

> We are paid daily, while they earn piece rate. When you help them to assemble the drawers, you aren't helping Cheng any more. The work they are doing is not part of our job any longer. It has been contracted out. You would just make their job easier. Besides, those women are young. They earn much more than I do.

While I was still trying very hard to understand why she brought up the topic and what the whole thing implied, Ms. Chang added, "Cheng didn't want to tell you about this. He doesn't want to make you feel bad." After this incident, whenever the outsiders appeared, I went back and forth between them and Ms. Chang to avoid any bad feelings.

## Gender Division of Labor in the Satellite Factory System

In addition to the less visible division between insiders and outsiders, there is a clear gender division of labor in the factories. Aggregated statistics show that married female workers were concentrated in small factories: between 1979 and 1988, around 55 percent of married women were employed in factories with fewer than thirty workers, whereas the majority of single women worked in factories with more than thirty workers (see Table 3.1). Married women are further handicapped by the

TABLE 3.1
Percentage Distribution of Female Workers in Factories of Different Sizes by Marital Status, Manufacturing, 1987

| Number of Employees | Single | Married | Divorced/ Widowed |
|---|---|---|---|
| 1 | 1.7 | 22.0 | 13.5 |
| 2–9 | 13.4 | 19.7 | 19.2 |
| 10–29 | 19.2 | 14.8 | 14.4 |
| 30–49 | 14.7 | 7.3 | 11.5 |
| 50–99 | 15.8 | 11.4 | 17.3 |
| 100–499 | 28.9 | 19.1 | 22.1 |
| 500 + | 6.3 | 5.7 | 1.9 |
| Total percentage | 100.0 | 100.0 | 99.9 |
| Total number of female workers | 1,055 | 1,195 | 104 |

SOURCE: Drawn from a nationwide survey of fertility and female labor-force participation conducted in 1987 by the Office of the Directorate-General of Budget, Accounting, and Statistics, Executive Yuan, R.O.C.

TABLE 3.2
Percentage Distribution of Type of Labor, Manufacturing, 1986

| | Total | Males | Females |
|---|---|---|---|
| Regular | 88.0 | 51.3 | 48.7 |
| Casual | 9.0 | 47.5 | 52.6 |
| Family member | 3.0 | 67.6 | 32.4 |
| Number of workers | 2,177,790 | 1,120,904 | 1,056,886 |

SOURCE: DGBAS (1988), Table 44, pp. 428–31.

likelihood that they will be hired as casual workers. Although there were slightly more men than women in the manufacturing sector in 1986, among the 9 percent of casual workers, women outnumbered men (see Table 3.2). Moreover, while factories with fewer than thirty workers only employed 17.5 percent of female workers, 24.2 percent of female casual workers worked for factories in this category (see Table 3.3). In other words, female casual workers are overrepresented in factories with fewer than thirty workers.

TABLE 3.3

Size of Factory by Gender and Type of Worker, Manufacturing, 1986 (in percentage)

| Number of Employees | Male | | | Female | | |
|---|---|---|---|---|---|---|
| | Regular | Causal | Total | Regular | Causal | Total |
| Less than 10 | 12.2 | 15.5 | 12.5 | 4.6 | 8.2 | 5.0 |
| 10–29 | 18.6 | 18.4 | 18.6 | 12.2 | 16.0 | 12.5 |
| 30–49 | 10.5 | 10.9 | 10.5 | 8.6 | 9.9 | 8.8 |
| 50–99 | 14.2 | 16.7 | 14.4 | 14.5 | 15.7 | 14.7 |
| 100–499 | 28.2 | 28.5 | 28.2 | 36.1 | 34.1 | 35.9 |
| 500+ | 16.4 | 10.1 | 15.8 | 24.0 | 16.1 | 23.3 |
| Total percentage | 100.1 | 100.1 | 100.0 | 100.0 | 100.0 | 100.2 |
| Total number of workers | 984,197 | 92,774 | | 933,102 | 102,726 | |

SOURCE: DGBAS (1988), Table 44, pp. 428–31.

The unfavorable nature of married women's job experiences can be further demonstrated by comparing the terms of employment of married women with those of single women, divorcees, and widows. Married women's labor is more likely to be unrewarded in monetary terms: in 1987, about one-tenth of married women worked as unpaid family workers as opposed to 1.5 percent or fewer of single, divorced, and widowed women (see Table 3.4). Although married women were more likely than single women to work as employers or self-employed workers, it was the divorced or widowed woman who, in the absence of a male household head, was most likely to take charge.

As a matter of fact, the likelihood that married women will work without pay increases dramatically when their husbands actually own a factory. As Table 3.5 shows, the majority of married women who participated in productive labor became unpaid family workers if their husbands were employers or self-employed workers; about one-third of the employers' wives and 52 percent of the wives of self-employed workers were unpaid family workers. The figures further show that the productive labor of women married to factory owners or self-employed workers is between thirty and fifty times more likely to be unrewarded (in monetary terms) than the labor of the wives of workers of private enterprises.

TABLE 3.4

Percentage Distribution of Female Workers' Employment Status by
Marital Status in Manufacturing, 1987

|  | Single | Married | Divorced/ Widowed |
|---|---|---|---|
| Employers | 0.2 | 0.9 | 1.9 |
| Self-employed workers | 0.2 | 1.5 | 3.9 |
| Private employees | 97.8 | 87.5 | 93.3 |
| Unpaid family workers | 1.8 | 10.0 | 1.0 |
| Total percentage | 100.0 | 100.0 | 100.0 |
| Total number of workers | 1,055 | 1,195 | 104 |

SOURCE: Drawn from a nationwide survey of fertility and female labor-force participation conducted in 1987 by the Office of the Directorate-General of Budget, Accounting,
and Statistics, Executive Yuan, R.O.C.

TABLE 3.5

Relationship between Married Women's Working Status and Their
Husbands' Employment Status in Manufacturing, 1987

| Wives | Husbands' Employment Status | | | |
|---|---|---|---|---|
|  | Employers | Self-Employed Workers | Private Employees | Unpaid Family Workers |
| Employers | 1.2 | — | 0.6 | 4.3 |
| Self-employed workers | 1.2 | 6.0 | 5.5 | 4.3 |
| Private employees | 12.8 | 7.5 | 41.5 | 4.3 |
| Unpaid family workers | 32.5 | 51.9 | 1.2 | 43.5 |
| Housewives | 52.1 | 34.6 | 50.8 | 43.5 |
| Total percentage | 99.8 | 100.0 | 99.6 | 99.9 |
| Total number of workers | 163 | 133 | 1,164 | 23 |

SOURCE: Drawn from a nationwide survey of fertility and female labor-force participation conducted in 1987 by the Office of the Directorate-General of Budget, Accounting,
and Statistics, Executive Yuan, R.O.C.

Ethnographic data I collected in factories producing wooden jewelry boxes confirm the aggregated statistics. Generally speaking, each factory employs only one or two skilled workers. The number of female workers depends on how many unskilled workers are needed. For example, in the box body factory, operating the electronic machines to do the cutting and carving requires skills that take a worker at least four to five years of training and experience to master. Typically, a box body factory consists of two male master workers (one of whom usually is the owner), one or two male apprentices, and several female assemblers. In most cases, the female assemblers are outsiders. In factories that only make doors/lids, drawers, or the front part of the drawers, the husband is usually the master, while the wife simultaneously does the assembling, moves the boxes around, cooks, and keeps an eye on their small children. Such factories may or may not hire another male worker to share the moving.

The organization of the painting and flannel factories is similar to that of the box body factory. The owner is usually the master worker who does the painting or cutting. He hires one or two male apprentices and several female workers to do the polishing, packing, or handling. The master worker in painting and flannel factories is less skilled. Generally speaking, a one-year apprentice can manage almost 70 percent of the work independently.

The glass factory needs a larger number of unskilled workers. After the master draws the design on the glass, different dyestuffs have to be filled in. Dyeing is known by the workers as "color painting" and makes up the major part of the work of a glass factory. Because many unskilled workers are needed and it is relatively easy to collect and distribute the pieces of glass, the glass factory recruits a large number of women doing homework in the neighborhood. The factory I stayed at normally employed fifteen to twenty homeworkers. This was true for the hardware factory as well. The latter hired large numbers of homeworkers to polish and pack the hinges, handles, screws, and other hardware.

In the assembly factory, there is only one skilled worker, the craftsmaster, who is capable of completing a wooden jewelry box from scratch on his own. His job is to produce new designs or modify old models. These models will be sent to the trading company for display. The rest of the workers in the assembly factory are unskilled. Compared to the work in other units in the production process, the work in the assembly factory is intensive and complex, involving more steps. The size of the labor force is therefore much larger than it is in other factories of the satellite factory system. The number of workers ranges from twenty to thirty. Among them, most are married women, who work as either insiders or outsiders.

In addition to gender and skill level, a number of other factors affect the composition of the workforce within each factory as well as the status and earning capacity of individual workers. In order to retain the complexity, I have compiled Tables 3.6 through 3.8. Factory 1 in Table 3.6 is an assembly factory where the owner, Mr. Li, was an aboriginal. When I worked in Mr. Li's factory in the summer of 1989, all the employees were aboriginal, except for two bookkeepers, worker 22, and her daughters who worked part-time (see Table 3.6, factory 1). Connections based on Mr. Li's own aboriginal background were strengthened further by family and kinship ties. The key figures of the factory—that is, the owner, manager, and craftsmaster—constituted the center of the network. Most of the other aboriginal workers were family members or distant relatives of these central individuals.

In both the assembly and box body factories, the majority (12 out of 14) of the female workers were married women, wives of the key figures or otherwise related to them. In contrast, the majority of the males were single. In factory 1, three of these men (the two retarded men and the alcoholic) were marginal individuals who under normal circumstances would have had a hard time finding employment in this society.

The kinship-based power structure within these factories was reinforced by the gender division of labor. The reasons why workers earned what they did differed greatly between men and women. As Table 3.6 shows, how much men earned was highly correlated with the work they did, for example, driving and delivering (worker 3) and painting (worker 9) in factory 1, craftsmaster (worker 4) and apprentice (worker 5) in factory 2. In contrast, the women's wages were determined by their relationships to the men. Among the women, the highest paid were the owner's and manager's wives (workers 1 and 2 in factory 1, and worker 1 in factory 2). Their relatives (workers 8 and 11) and the craftsmaster's wife (worker 12) in factory 1 earned somewhat less. Besides, all the highest paid, skilled jobs (except quality control in factory 1) went to men.

To ensure a sufficient and stable labor supply during the peak sea-

TABLE 3.6
Labor Relations and Gender Division of Labor in the Satellite Factory System—Insiders

| Title | Gender, Marital Status* | Wages | Social Relations | Major Responsibilities | Winter 1989 |
|---|---|---|---|---|---|
| **Factory 1** | | | | | |
| Owner | MM | NA | | | |
| Partner | FM | NA | Owner's brother's wife | | |
| Bookkeeper 1 | FM | NA | Husband is a representative of a trading company | Subcontracting and bookkeeping | |
| Bookkeeper 2 | FS | NA | Cousin of Bookkeeper 1's classmate | Bookkeeping | Left |
| Manager | MM | NA | Partner | | |
| Craftsmaster | MM | $600 | Worker 2's cousin | Craftsmaster | |
| Worker 1 | FM | $355 | Owner's wife | Cooking, monitoring, assembling | |
| Worker 2 | FM | $350 | Manager's wife | Assembling | |
| Worker 3 | MS | $460 | Worker 1's cousin | Driving and delivering | |
| Worker 4 | FM | $315 | Worker 1's brother's wife | Assembling | Absent |
| Worker 5 | FS | $280 | Worker 1's fellow villager | Assembling | Absent |
| Worker 6 | FM | $280 | Manager's brother's wife | Assembling | Absent |
| Worker 7 | MS | $350 | Worker 2's brother | Assembling and moving boxes | |
| Worker 8 | FM | $295 | Worker 2's sister | Assembling | Absent |
| Worker 9 | MM | $425 | Worker 8's husband | Assembling and painting | Absent |

| Worker | Status | Wage | Relationship | Task | Notes |
|---|---|---|---|---|---|
| Worker 10 | FM | $295 | Worker 2's brother's wife | Assembling | Absent |
| Worker 11 | MS | $230 | Craftsmaster's cousin | Assembling | Absent |
| Worker 12 | FM | $285 | Craftsmaster's wife | Assembling | |
| Worker 13 | MS | $400 | Owner's neighboring tribe | Assembling | Left |
| Worker 14 | MS | $230 | Worker 13's younger brother | Assembling | Left |
| Worker 15 | MS | $230 | Worker 13's friend | Assembling | Left |
| Worker 16 | MS | $230 | Worker 13's friend | Assembling | Left |
| Worker 17 | MS | $200 | Owner's tribe (mentally retarded) | Moving boxes around | |
| Worker 18 | MS | $210 | Owner's tribe (mentally retarded) | Moving boxes around | |
| Worker 19 | MS | $350 | Owner's tribe (an alcoholic) | Repairing defective items | Absent |
| Worker 20 | FS | $230 | Owner's tribe | Assembling | Absent |
| Worker 21 | FM | $280 | Owner's tribe | Assembling | Absent |
| Worker 22 | FM | $330 | Lives next door to the factory | Quality control | |
| Worker 23 | FS | $180 | Worker 22's daughter, part-time | Assembling | Absent |
| Worker 24 | FS | $150 | Worker 22's daughter, part-time | Assembling | Absent |

### Factory 2: Box Body Factory

| Worker | Status | Wage | Relationship |
|---|---|---|---|
| Owner | MM | $800 | |
| Worker 1 | FM | $500 | Owner's wife |
| Worker 2 | FM | $400 | Woman in the same village |
| Worker 3 | FM | $400 | Matchmaker in the village |
| Worker 4 | MS | $670 | Craftsmaster |
| Worker 5 | MS | $500 | Apprentice, an aborigine |

*MM: male and married; MS: male and single; FM: female and married; FS: female and single.

SOURCE: Field notes

son, some factories give bonuses to workers who can bring in other workers. Thus worker 13 in factory 1 received a substantially higher level of wages because he came to work in this factory with three others (workers 15, 16, and 17). The higher level of wages was subsequently used to ensure that he, and therefore his group, would stay. Managers and owners told me about several incidents where the factory's production was temporarily interrupted because a group of workers quit unexpectedly with its leader.

Family and kinship ties also serve as essential bonds among the outsiders. In Table 3.7, group 1 comprised three workers, Ms. Wu and two teenagers, Aching and Aling, whose job was to glue the interior flannel into the boxes. A large quantity of the work, usually several thousand pieces per contract, was contracted out by Ms. Wu's husband. Aching and Aling are brother and sister. Their parents were friends of Mr. and Ms. Wu. Group 2 comprised four to five workers who screwed the hangers, doors/lids, and handles to the boxes. In Hong-fu, a box body factory where doors/lids and drawers were made, Ashiea and her three sisters-in-law (i.e., group 3) worked as outsiders who glued various pieces of wooden boards together into drawers or doors. Apart from the male subcontractors in groups 1 and 2, the majority of the outsiders were married women. Group 3 differed from the other two in that it did not have a subcontractor. The four sisters-in-law contracted work out from the factories themselves. Instead of getting monthly wages, they divided the earnings at the end of each month. In the local community, they were known as tough and lucky women.

For married women who worked as homeworkers, community networks proved to be more important than family and kinship ties in getting jobs (see Table 3.8). Except for the mother-in-law, all these homeworkers had small children in their households.

In addition to generating profits through an ample labor supply in the peak season, factory owners cut costs by dramatically decreasing their labor force to minimum in the off-season. During my revisit in the winter of 1989, none of the outsiders and homeworkers were employed. One assembly factory had completely shut down its operation. The glass, box body, hardware, and another assembly factories only kept their insiders. Mr. Li's factory continued to operate with less than 40 percent of its peak-season labor force, having excluded all the outsiders (see Table 3.6, right-hand column). It is by drastically cutting labor costs in this way that the owners can generate maximum profits.

TABLE 3.7

Labor Relations and Gender Division of Labor in the Satellite Factory System—Outsiders

| Group 1 | Gender, Marital Status* | Social Relations |
|---|---|---|
| **Group 1** | | |
| Worker 1 | MM | Subcontractor |
| Worker 2 | FM | Subcontractor's wife |
| Worker 3 | MS | Subcontractor's friend's teenage son |
| Worker 4 | FS | Worker 3's younger sister |
| **Group 2** | | |
| Worker 1 | MM | Subcontractor |
| Worker 2 | FM | Subcontractor's wife |
| Worker 3 | FM | Subcontractor's mother |
| Worker 4 | FM | Worker 1's neighbor |
| Worker 5 | FM | Worker 1's neighbor |
| **Group 3** | | |
| Worker 1 | FM | Worker 2's sister-in-law; her husband is the brother of worker 2's husband |
| Worker 2 | FM | Worker 1's sister-in-law |
| Worker 3 | FM | Her husband is the cousin of worker 1's and worker 2's husbands |
| Worker 4 | FM | Same as worker 3 |

*MM: male and married; MS: male and single; FM: female and married; FS: female and single.
SOURCE: Field notes

## Conclusions

I began this chapter by discussing structural constraints imposed on manufacturers involved in Taiwan's export-led economy. Fierce competition and a low survival rate among local producers suggest that proletarians who aspire to upward mobility do not have a good chance to succeed. The satellite factory system thus serves to mobilize local re-

TABLE 3.8

Labor Relations and Gender Division of Labor in the Satellite Factory System—Homeworkers

| | Gender, Marital Status* | Social Relations |
|---|---|---|
| Worker 1 | FM | The neighbor of an ex-homeworker |
| Worker 2 | FM | The upstairs neighbor of worker 1 |
| Worker 3 | FM | The next-door neighbor of worker 2 |
| Worker 4 | FM | The daughter-in-law of a peddler who sells cold drinks in the neighborhood |
| Worker 5 | FM | The daughter-in-law of a landlord who used to rent an apartment to the factory owner |
| Worker 6 | FM | Worker 5's neighbor |
| Worker 7 | FM | Wife of the owner's brother |
| Worker 8 | FM | Neighbor of worker 7 |
| Worker 9 | FM | Worker 8's mother-in-law |

*MM: male and married; MS: male and single; FM: female and married; FS: female and single.
SOURCE: Field notes

sources to produce for international markets while simultaneously passing on the detrimental effects of international constraints to small production units in local communities. Factory owners rely on the system to realize labor control, increase productivity, and call on reserve labor. Their calculated deployment of insiders, outsiders, and homeworkers enables them to avoid any long-term obligation to those from whom they reap profit.

The statistical data show that the "economic miracle," based on the satellite factory system, has given more Taiwanese men an opportunity to become owners or self-employed workers. Women, however, have been incorporated into the system primarily as unpaid family workers, wage workers, or casual homeworkers. For men, the possibility of opening one's own factory has been a way to resist the overall trend of proletarianization induced by economic development. However, the untold story behind this countermovement is the perpetuation of gender inequality. In particular, the productive labor of women married to factory owners is more likely to be unrewarded, in monetary terms, than is the labor of the wives of workers in private enterprises.

In Taiwanese the owner of a small factory is called a *taogei*. The same words denote "head of the household." The fact that a proletarian may become the owner of a small factory means that a large number of household heads have had a chance to enhance their authority within the family through their ownership of the means of production.[4] The presence of an "inflated petty bourgeoisie" means that the foundations of the patriarchal family system have been reinforced. A large percentage of the male petty bourgeoisie can thus legitimate their control over their wives through the control of capital. Therefore, it is not possible to understand Taiwan's economic development without taking the interplay of class and gender into account.

# 4

# Women, Marriage, and Family in the Satellite Factory System

So far, we have discussed the sociopolitical environment within which married women are employed as well as the organization of the satellite system in terms of gender. Now it is time to examine more closely the mechanisms through which married women are molded into mothers, wives, and daughters-in-law on the one hand, and waged, unwaged, and causal workers on the other. I will use women's stories of their first years of marriage to illustrate how women themselves understand and reflect upon their own experiences of this conversion process, and then discuss the clash between women's gender and class identities.

## Marriage: The Ultimate Destiny!

Before we enter into these women's married lives, it is necessary to explain why the majority of factory daughters in Taiwan perceive marriage as their ultimate destiny and to examine the conditions under which they enter marriage. Statistics show that, even though there has been a postponement of marriage in recent years, the majority of Taiwanese women do eventually get married. In 1983 about 90 percent of women between the ages 30 and 34 were married, and more than 90 percent of the age group 35 to 39 (Liu Yu-lan 1985, 78). These figures are the outcome of the pull-and-push forces that make family life an attractive choice for individuals in Chinese society. Both men and women are pulled into family life. For a man, this is the only legitimate means to fulfil his obligation to carry on his family lineage. For a woman, having a family ensures that when she dies her soul will be worshipped, eliminating the possibility that it might become a ghost wandering the countryside.[1] Besides, there are practical concerns in everyday life that make remaining single unappealing in Chinese society. For one thing, the conjugal pair is the fundamental social unit. Leisure activities, consumer products, and housing construction are all organized around, or designed for, individuals belonging to family units. Furthermore, unmarried individuals are stigmatized as deviant or immature adults.

A Chinese proverb says, "*Nanda danghun, nuda dangjia*," meaning that both men and women should get married on reaching adulthood. The age at which women are expected to marry varies according to their socioeconomic background and has changed over the past decades.[2] Generally speaking, women aged 25 or over who lack a committed relationship are considered as people at risk. Single women experience tremendous pressure around age 28 and 29, because women after 30 are labeled *laochunu,* meaning "spinsters" (Zheng and Liao 1985, 135; *Zhongguo Luntan,* 1982). Indeed, in an article discussing the psychological aspects of being a single woman, the author uses the term *yuling weihun,* meaning "over the acceptable marriage age," to describe single women who are over 30 (Ding 1984, 18). Another very popular female newspaper columnist once warned her young female readers not to give in rashly to the new fashion of being "single nobles," as unmarried female elites are popularly called:

> When you have the opportunity to fall in love and have a romance, don't refuse or run away from it. When you have the opportunity to get married, don't scorn it. I have seen so many young girls who have changed from being very picky about potential partners to longing for one [and yet being unable to find any]. How painful it is! How pitiful they are! . . . Family life may seem to be very conventional, but we need to know who we are before we can know if we ourselves can afford to be unconventional. Nowadays, women are given more choices, since marriage is no longer the only career for women. However, the women need to have the wisdom to make a decision. (Weiwei Furen 1987, 17)

The desirability of having a family and becoming a wife and mother is accentuated by the stigma commonly associated with divorce. Despite the gradual increase in the divorce rate in recent years, divorce is nonetheless considered a pernicious result of declining moral standards, a negative product of industrialization, and both cause and symptom of a dissolving family system. Female divorcees are discriminated against in employment and excluded from social activities (Arrigo 1984, 132–43;

Shi 1987).[3] In fact, the limited impact of feminist organizations or movements on the majority of the women in Taiwan has been attributed to the "bad records" of their leaders, many of whom are either single or divorced (M.-J. Li 1987, 253).

Even though getting married to form a family is the norm, young women are not well prepared for their new roles after marriage. In Taiwan, as in many other countries, single women have only a very vague idea about what marriage and family life really involve (Rubin 1976). They are not ready for the transition from the single to the married state. Hardly any sex education is provided in Taiwan's schools. Sexual knowledge among youth ranges from "poor" or "inadequate" to "incorrect." (Yen 1989, 292–93). Many studies show that, by the time they graduate, high school or junior high school students can only answer correctly one-half to two-thirds of questions on sexuality and reproduction (Yen 1989, 292–93). Female students appear to be even less informed than their male counterparts (Cemada et al. 1986).[4] In a study on the family-planning education of female factory workers, researchers found that about one-third of the married women knew nothing about birth control when they first had intercourse, and about 70 percent of them did not use contraceptives at that time. There was a great unfilled demand among factory girls for information on sex, on how to interact with men before marriage, and on family life after marriage (Hsiung, Wang, and Lu 1989, 187).

Young factory girls who entered the job market in the 1970s, when Taiwan was first incorporated into the international market, generally regarded marriage as a route to upward mobility. Both factory daughters and their mothers believed that the factory jobs would make a real difference for their future prospects (Kung 1976). They based their conjugal fantasies about their boyfriends, weddings, and married life on novels, television, movies, and women's magazines. The romanticized middle-class family presented in the mass media fed these young women's urge to escape from their current factory life (Diamond 1979, 327–34). There was vicious competition among them for potential husbands, especially in the textile or electronics factories where women made up the majority of the employees (Arrigo 1984; Yang 1977). Factory girls were often reported as the victims of sexual abuse or harassment, and premarital pregnancy was not infrequent (Ziping 1982; Yang 1976). The majority of factory girls said that they preferred not to continue working at their factory jobs after marriage (Diamond 1979, 327–28). Employment did give the young women more say about their marriage. That is, they were now free not to marry a given man. Yet, those who went so far as to insist upon personally choosing whom they wanted to marry ran the risk of permanently breaking ties with their natal families (Kung 1983).

In the following section, I draw on one matchmaker's perception of marriage and family to illuminate the changing expectations of married women in Taiwan. My rationale is that, during periods of transition, practices or events that are traditionally important to the local community will undergo a transformation in meaning. The matchmaker's continuing involvement in matchmaking while holding her factory job is a good example of how conventional practices are adapted to accomplish multiple goals in a changing world. Her narratives show clearly how she makes sense of the social reality surrounding her.

## A Matchmaker's Perspective

In Chinese society, marriage permits the formation, strengthening, and consolidation of social ties. Aside from the bride's and groom's families, matchmakers traditionally play the most active roles at such times. In the local communities, they not only possess virtuoso social skills but very often are at the center of information networks. Though nowadays more and more young people make initial contact with their marital partners themselves, matchmakers are still frequently approached by people in the community. In addition to their conventional role as go-betweens, matchmakers are now increasingly seen as the authorities on marriage rituals. They are invited to oversee the entire wedding ceremony to make sure that no taboo is violated. At both engagement and wedding ceremonies, a matchmaker is a symbol of good fortune; it is she who brings together the young couples who will carry on the lineage name and family traditions.

Ms. Chow, a matchmaker who now works in a box body factory, told me what makes her continue to act as a matchmaker in the local community.

> It's really fun. In a community like this, if you talk to people often,
> you know which family's daughter is ready to marry out and which
> family is ready to get a daughter-in-law. Sometimes people just come
> to me for help. I don't even need to ask around. Everyone knows that
> I am a reliable matchmaker. I know what to say and what not to say. I
> don't upset people. If it works out, both families thank me with

*hongbao* [tips in a red envelope]. If it [the newly married couple's first child] is a son, they bring me *yufan* (gourmet rice for special occasions) and a bottle of wine. Things really go well in this way.

When I asked her how much she gets in a *hongbao,* she replied,

Between ten thousand and twenty thousand. It varies. The groom's family usually gives me more than the bride's family. It's really not bad. [It's a business in which] you don't need to put in money. Also you don't need to labor yourself. What more could you ask for? It's really a job you can do for a long time. It doesn't take that much out of you. You can do it even when you get really old.

This narrative reveals the pride and satisfaction a matchmaker shares with the families involved in a marriage, the reward she receives if the married couple enjoys the *blessing* of a male child, and the delightful privilege a matchmaker enjoys in her local community.[5] Most significantly, the matchmaking brings Chow tangible revenue, in comparison with her monthly wages of NT$12,000 to 15,000 in the factory. The distinction Chow made between her factory job and her matchmaking activities bears witness to a major social change: Matchmaking has existed for a long time, but wage-earning factory jobs are new. As a factory worker, Chow has to perform physical labor in exchange for wages, while as a matchmaker, she relies exclusively on her social skills and community networks. This is an instance of new wine filling an old bottle.

The conjunction of factory work and matchmaking actually facilitates both. During the time I was doing my fieldwork, Chow made an effort to introduce one of the nieces in her extended family to her boss, the factory owner. When they got engaged, she was very pleased. On our way to the ceremony, she told me, "Now he [the factory owner] should call me aunt!"

On another occasion, when the factory craftsmaster did not show up for two days, the factory owner told me he might try to solve the problem by getting help from the matchmaker. He said that he had talked to Chow about this problem.

He [the craftsmaster] has been in a bad mood. His girlfriend just broke up with him. He wants to quit. I have asked Chow to introduce young women around here to him. . . . She is really a good matchmaker. She is not the traditional type of matchmaker. She doesn't just leave them [the young people] on their own after introducing them. She always arranges things for them so that they have a chance to meet and know each other. . . . If he gets married, he will be more reliable. Besides, getting married with someone around here would be good. He will become a member of the village.

## The Transition to Married Life

Married women I met in the field often described their premarriage perceptions of married life as naive. The transition to the married state is a difficult one for many women. It is a matter of being made over into a mother, wife, and daughter-in-law. For A-in, a piece-rate worker in her mid-thirties, this transition involved learning to shoulder laborious housework.

> After I was introduced to my husband, a coworker asked me if I was concerned about becoming the older sister-in-law in a family of seven brothers. I told her that didn't bother me at all. I said that there was nothing to worry about. After the engagement, I cam to visit my husband's house. I did the dishes after lunch. That scared the hell out of me. The bowls were piled up this high, and the dishes were all over. I went back to my coworker and told her I was really worried. But it was too late. I took up all the family chores once I stepped into this family. Every morning I got up around four o'clock. It took me at least a half hour to start the fire. I watched the rice cooking while going back and forth between the well and the kitchen. I needed to carry enough water to the house for the entire day's use. After the rice was ready, I needed to cook several dishes for breakfast and prepare my husband's brothers' lunch boxes. I had to prepare six lunch boxes back then. You could never imagine how hard it is to become a daughter and sister-in-law in a big family like this. I was so naive when I was single.

For Ms. Lin, who was in charge of inventory control and bookkeeping in a hardware factory, being a daughter-in-law meant being forced to cut her ties with the natal family. As the only daughter of her parents, Ms. Lin got married at age twenty-five through an arranged marriage. When she talked about her married life, she said,

> I really don't have much freedom. During all these years I have been married, they have only let me visit home twice, once when my grandfather died and another time when my father-in-law got mad at my husband. He kicked my husband, the kids, and me out. My husband ended up staying in a hotel. My kids and I went back to my parents' house. I know my parents have been missing me very much. I

was their only daughter. When they arranged the marriage for me, my mother didn't want me to marry somebody who lived far away. Nobody ever thought that even though we live so close to each other, we still wouldn't get to see each other. . . . Once my father waited around the corner of the street I usually take to work in the morning, just to see me pass by. When he told me this later on the phone, I cried. I know they miss me very much. . . . I didn't know it would be so difficult to be a daughter-in-law.

When I realized that Ms. Lin's parents lived only fifteen minutes away from where she now lives, I asked her what would happen if she were to visit them without the in-laws' permission. She replied, "As a daughter-in-law, you can't do things that you want. It just doesn't work that way."

The story of Feng-yuan, a twenty-nine-year-old homeworker, is a mix of disappointments that she experienced as she took up her responsibilities as a mother and wife. When we talked about her marriage, she actually began by telling me about an abortive romance that preceded her current marriage. The earlier courtship ended because of pressures from her father. He insisted that Feng-yuan stop dating the boyfriend because he shared her surname.[6] Feng-yuan was then introduced to the man who became her husband. He turned out to be a gambler. In retrospect, Feng-yuan believed, "Before getting married, we girls were really spoiled. We acted as if we were princesses. After getting married, we realized what real life truly means." When I asked what marriage meant to her, she replied,

> Getting married really doesn't guarantee anything. If the marriage goes well, you are lucky. Otherwise, it can almost destroy your whole life. Especially after your children have been born, you feel like there is no way out. I tell myself all the time that I have to be patient. In order to give my daughter a happy childhood, I have to be patient. Sometimes I wonder if there really is an end to all of this. . . . Although I have hardly any affection left for the marriage, I have been a responsible wife and mother.

Contrary to the experiences of rural women in Margery Wolf's work, married women working in the satellite factories can no longer rely upon the "uterine family" they created for emotional and financial security. Lao-er, a tailor who came to work in her brother's factory in the peak season, talked with much despair and sadness about her marriage, her role as a mother, and what it means to be a woman:

The first year of my marriage, things were fine. After that, he changed. Others think I was naive to have a second child. I was hoping that he would come back. Now I realize it's impossible to get him back. . . . He never brings any money home. I pay for everything. After he moved out, I really didn't have a marriage anymore. Except for having two kids to care for, I am just like a single woman. . . . My father always says there is evil karma following me. . . . In a way, I feel I am lucky. I am a tailor. I don't need to rely on him. . . . To put it nicely, I would say that I must have owed him a lot in my previous life. Now he is simply reclaiming the debts. On the other hand, I may say, "How come I was so unfortunate as to meet a guy like him?" . . . Before I converted to Buddhism, I really had a hard time accepting all of this. Whenever I thought about what had happened to me, I cried. With these two kids, I have to take care of everything. Several times I really thought about putting an end to all the suffering. Now I take it more lightly. Maybe this is what life is supposed to be like. . . . I just don't resist. I let it go. I take care of the kids and try to make the best out of it. . . . Among the customers I make clothes for, six or seven out of ten have to raise their kids on their own. I really don't understand why marriage turns out like this.

These narratives suggest that the women were extraordinarily naive before they married. I do not have data to explain why this is so. Many of them should have seen what happened to their sisters-in-law or their own sisters when they first married. The fact remains that almost all women in their thirties expressed such sentiments when they spoke about their first years of marriage. Clearly, there is considerable emotional trauma as single women are converted into married women and are forced to adapt to their new roles as wives, mothers, and daughters-in-law.

## Adjustment to the Working World

In the past, women's distressful experiences in the first years of their marriage were mainly due to their new roles as mothers, wives, and daughters-in-law. For married women employed in Taiwan's satellite factories, the trauma is compounded as they undergo the process that molds them into waged, unwaged, or casual workers. The satellite factory system represents the latest version of the Chinese family, one in which the patriarchal order is called upon for capitalist production.

When a man is thinking of getting married, he calculates how much he will have to spend for the engagement party, bride price, and wedding, and how much of his investment will be recouped when the wife joins the labor force. When I congratulated Cheng, an owner of a box body factory, on his forthcoming engagement, he talked about his bride-to-be. His statement bluntly attests the roles young women are expected to take on once they are married.

> I don't intend to get a decorative vase. I am not aiming for sex either. If I want sex, I can get cheap sex on the street. I heard that she is very good at bookkeeping. People say that she is really thrifty, and hardworking too. The other day, I ran into her in the market. She was riding a 125-cc motorcycle. You know, she is really physically very strong.

When I asked him how much he had to spend in total, he said it will be about NT$400,000. "It's worth it. People think I have a pretty good deal, you know," said Cheng.

Concerns of productive labor in the factory and reproductive labor in the family now are closely intertwined in Taiwan's satellite manufacturing system. From the owner's standpoint, women's labor, both productive and reproductive, is essential. A matchmaker once explained why it was important for a factory owner to get married.

> So that you get someone to do the cleaning, cooking, and laundry. A woman makes it look more like a real family. Besides, if he has to take care of everything all by himself, he won't be able to make any money. The business will go nowhere. It just won't expand.

Expecting married women to combine multiple roles is a new development. Women married to factory owners often did not know—or, at least, did not fully realize—that they were expected to fulfill the dual roles of worker and married women. It is emotionally trying for married women to figure out what is involved in their new roles. Only through mistakes and embarrassment does a woman come to learn how to juggle between these two domains. Lu, a woman in her early thirties, talked about the difficulties she had to go through in her first years of marriage. She finished elementary school and decided not to continue because she was convinced that she did not know enough to pass the entry examination for junior high school. She worked in a garment factory in the Tan-zi Export Processing Zone for more than ten years. Her marriage was arranged by her parents. When she married, she had to quit her job because the factory run by her husband's family needed her labor. Recalling her early married life, she said,

After our engagement, I came to visit his family once. I was really naive at that time. I saw they had so many rooms in the house. I worried about how long it was going to take to do the cleaning every time. I never thought of what it meant to marry into a family with a factory and so many sons. I was young and simpleminded. I didn't know that I was expected to work in the factory. . . . Several days after my wedding, I started working in the factory. At that time, my sister-in-law [husband's older brother's wife] did the cooking. She didn't do factory work. Around noon, we were called to have lunch. I didn't think twice. I just sat down and ate. My sister-in-law sat to one side feeding her son. My mother-in-law sat next to my sister-in-law chatting. The first few days, I wasn't aware of anything. I just sat down and ate. After a while, I started to feel strange. I came to realize that they [the in-laws] were waiting, that women were supposed to wait until their husbands and sons finished the meal first. I became very nervous and uncomfortable. I didn't have a kid to play with while I waited. Besides, I had to get back to work in the afternoon. . . . Dinner time was easier. After finishing the factory work in the afternoon, I immediately went to boil water for showers. After I had taken a shower, I stayed in my room upstairs. I waited until they were about to finish their dinner, then I came down. Sometimes I heard my mother-in-law say out loud, "How come it takes so long for that woman to take a shower!" She was concerned about how much water I used. In fact, I was just waiting in my room and trying to avoid the awkwardness of sitting there with them not knowing what to do. . . . The year after my wedding was the most difficult time in my whole life. I will never forget it for the rest of my life. . . . Every day I got nervous when the mealtime approached. . . . After my son was born, things became easier. I had a son to feed while waiting.

Lu explained how she combined her child-rearing responsibility with the labor she was expected to contribute to the factory owned by her husband's family.

I started working in the factory again when my son was one month old. I didn't take that much time off. When I went to visit my mother, she scolded me: she thought I should have rested for at least two months. . . . I put him in a roller cart and tied the cart to my machine. He was a very nice baby. I pulled the cart back and forth with the string connected to my machine to keep him from crying. I fed him once in the morning and once at noon. He usually slept through the morning and afternoon. In general, he was easy to care for. People say that he is the kind of kid who knows his fate from the beginning. He knew that I had to work, that his mother could not care for him full-time. When

> my second son was born, I put both of them in the cart. Sometimes, the older one tried to take care of the baby. . . . At that time, the business was going very well. We had to work overtime all the time.

A year before I met her, the family business slowed down. Lu's full-time labor was no longer needed in the factory. She started looking for jobs elsewhere. Even after she found a job in a neighborhood hardware factory, she had to compensate for the unpaid labor she no longer contributed to the family factory by coming up with a special work arrangement:

> Lu's scheduled starts around 7:00 in the morning. She has to get ready for work by 7:15. Before leaving home for her paid job, she first works in the family factory for thirty minutes. She and her two sisters-in-law also take weekly turns cooking for the family factory. Lu works for wages in a hardware store from 8:00 to 12:00 only during the weeks when her two sisters-in-law cook lunch. In other weeks she leaves Sing-liang at 11:00 and gets back at 12:30 instead of at 1:00 P.M. when other workers come back from their lunch. After the paid work, she works in the family factory again from 4:30 to 5:30. Lu is paid hourly by the hardware store because she does not work 40 hours every week.

Married women's unwaged labor is part of the human resources a start-up factory draws upon. Show-may had met her husband at Ta-you several years previously. After they got married, her husband and a friend decided to start a factory themselves. Show-may left Ta-you to work in the new factory. She got pregnant within a year. "At that time, it was really hard," Show-may said.

> The business had just got started. They [her husband and the friend] always worked until one or two o'clock in the morning. I stayed up late with them and cooked snacks for them after they had finished the work.

Throughout their career in the satellite factories, married women need to combine their factory work with child-rearing responsibilities. They must either go back and forth between factory work and homework or bring their children along to work. No matter what arrangement is made, the main issue for married women is to attach themselves to the system informally so that extra money can be earned during their child-rearing period.

In a small glass factory I visited, an indigenous worker told me that she had been working there for four years. She had a three-year-old son and two-month-old daughter. After her son was born, she successfully persuaded the owner to let her bring the baby to work. She fed her baby once in the morning and once in the afternoon. Two months previously, she had given birth to her second child. Now she was bringing both her children to the factory. While she worked, her son played with the owner's daughter, who was three and a half. The two-month-old girl slept in the cart next to her. The woman felt that she had been really lucky because the glass factory was small (there is only one other wage worker in the factory) and the owner and his wife had been very considerate. She said, "Most factories would not have allowed me to continue to work, not to mention bring my kids with me every day."

A-lang worked as an outsider with a group of seven or eight workers. The day I met her in the factory, she had her seven-year-old son and three-year-daughter with her. The son had not gone to school that day because he had a cold. As we worked, the children jumped up and down on the worktable. The next day A-lang only brought her daughter. Before the work got started, A-lang put a brushed cardboard box on the floor for her daughter to sleep on. A-lang old me that she had returned to factory work only recently. Before, she had worked as a homeworker for years while her children were small; her husband had brought contracted work home for her.

Once they get back to the factory job, women adopt extremely complicated daily schedules to accommodate their multiple responsibilities. They need to be flexible enough to constantly shift from one task to another, but also precise and disciplined enough to accomplish each task within the particular time slot.

Feng-yuan, the gambler's wife, paints stained glass at a sweatshop five doors away from her apartment. While her husband was employed, Feng-yuan would arrive at the sweatshop by 8:00 in the morning, after her husband left for work. At around 11:00, she would go back to her apartment to prepare lunch for him. After her husband returned to work around one o'clock, she would come back to work until 5:30 or 6:00, when she went home to prepare dinner. After dinner, she continued to paint glass at home while she waited for water to arrive, to do the family laundry or other chores. She did not go to sleep until after midnight. Feng-yuan continued to work at the sweatshop and to take care of her home even when her husband was unemployed and spent the nights gambling. The only difference was that her eyes were often red from crying.

In another case, A-in, the woman who married into a family with seven sons, and her second sister-in-law (her husband's second brother's wife) took turns staying at home to look after their father-in-law, who had been confined to bed for the last ten years. As a member of the outsiders, she could only work in the factory from one to three o'clock in the afternoon, when her father-in-law took his nap. As soon as he fell asleep, A-in would rush into the factory, squat on the floor and remove as many of the rubber bands used to hold in place the newly glued drawers as she possibly could. The whole time she did this, she never talked. Only upon departure did she say good-bye. Another member of the group, A-hsia, also had a father-in-law she cared for. She and her sister-in-law divided the responsibility: each took care of him for fifteen days a month. When it was A-hsia's turn, she got up around 6:00 and prepared both breakfast and lunch for him before she came to work, because he insisted on eating his noon meal at 11:45. A-hsia went home at 12:00 to eat the leftovers. She returned to the factory at 12:50 and went home to cook dinner at around 5:10. After dinner, she used to go back to work in the factory until 9:00 P.M.

In the past, when a Chinese woman got married, there was a period of adjustment during which her new identities as wife, mother, and daughter-in-law were developed within the domain of patriarchal order. The latest version of Chinese family life imposes additional demands. Under the satellite factory system, women's labor within the marriage is incorporated into the factory system. The underlying mechanisms of such incorporation are the patriarchal order as well as the operation of capitalism. Women's unflagging efforts to coordinate their productive and reproductive labor illustrate the coercive aspects of these two forces. On the surface, women *choose* to work in the small satellite factories in their neighborhoods. In essence, this is the only way married women can fulfill the latest multiple expectations of a married working-class woman: a responsible mother, dutiful wife, filial daughter-in-law, and hardworking worker. In contrast, women who are married to the factory owners are caught by the tension between their affiliation to the petty capitalist and their membership in an inferior class defined according to the patriarchal order.

The following three sections further elaborate on what it means to women that the productive system into which they are incorporated is small in scale, family centered, and export oriented. I use women's own words as headings to highlight the underlying theme of each section.

## "Husbands Enjoy a Better Life!"

Once I began talking to my female coworkers about their marriage and family lives, it became clear that the women were very aware of and quite frank about their inferior status. Although the way these women articulated the issue varied, the general consensus was "Husbands enjoy a better life," as the wife of a factory owner put it. In their daily lives, women learn to accommodate the practical differences between men and women, differences defined by the patriarchal order. Women perceive this order as a reality that they cannot change. A-lang, one of the outsiders, stated,

> When I go to work, I have to take my daughter with me. At home, my husband either watches TV or takes a nap after he finishes a day of work. To me, leaving the factory doesn't mean my work is done. [After dinner] I have to take care of the kids, bathe them, and wash clothes.

When Show-may got into an argument with a male worker on the subject of the differences between men and women, she said,

> Men and women are not equal at all. Men fool around [have affairs or go to prostitutes] even after they get married. Women can never do things like that, whether they are married or not. Besides, it's the women who have to take care of the kids. . . . Don't argue with me. The fact that men and women aren't equal is a reality. There is no way you can win [in arguing with me on this subject].

The fact that Taiwanese women are not blind to patriarchal ideology is also reported by Ian Skoggard among female workers in the shoe industry. On one occasion Skoggard asked female workers why they were working so late into the evening. Skoggard states, "One of them responded, 'because we are dumb.' We all laughed" (Skoggard 1993, 158).

Some women never forget the dreams they have been forced to give up and the compromises they have eventually come to make. Lao-er, the tailor, expressed what she felt she had gone through.

> We women really have difficult lives. After you get married and have kids, you have to give up a lot. Many of the things you really want to do, you now have to give up because of the family and kids.

During a conversation with Lin, the woman who had visited her natal family only twice in her fourteen years of marriage, I learned how she reconciled the world around her.

"Today I got up late. It was about six o'clock already. Usually I get up around five. Every day I sweep the floor; I either do it after I go home or after dinner. I mop the floor twice a week. Most of the time, I do this in the morning before anybody gets up. I wash the clothes by hand. Otherwise my husband would complain, saying that the clothes aren't clean enough. I use the washer only for some heavy winter clothes. I iron all the clothes every other day."

"How long does all the work take?" I asked, "Doesn't it take a long time?"

"No, it doesn't take that long. I have gotten used to it," replied Lin.

"How come you do all of this by yourself?" I asked again.

"Because we are housewives," answered Lin.

"But you also have a job!" I commented.

"Job is what I do outside. When I get home, I am still a housewife," explained Lin. As she put it in another conversation, "When I was young, I didn't think that much. I was very simpleminded. After getting married, I've came to realize that things can be very complicated."

## "I'm Not Just Making Pocket Money!"

One of the institutionalized assumptions of the satellite factory system is that every household has a male breadwinner. Women's primary role as mothers and wives are used as an excuse to incorporate married women into the satellite factory system not as "regular" workers but as homeworkers and secondary earners. This practice not only imposes limits on women's ability to improve their status through employment, but also ignores the fact that a household may not always have a breadwinner. The following incident illustrates the pressures married women experience if the institutionalized assumption of the ever-present breadwinner is not realized.

When I visited Feng-yuan, the gambler's wife, I learned that her husband had been unemployed for about three weeks. Show-pao, another woman in the neighborhood, stopped by the sweatshop. Feng-yuan said to her, "It has been twenty days."

Show-pao was surprised. "Really? I thought it had only been two weeks. Do you know what really happened? Was he laid off or was it his own idea to quit?"

"I don't know," Feng-yuan replied. "He never tells me what's going on. I really wish he would just disappear or even die."

Show-pao comforted Feng-yuan, "Don't say thing likes that. Men are all the same. The guy in my house [Show-pao's husband] is not any better."

"At least you don't have to raise the whole family," Feng-yuan responded. "Others are women. I too am a woman. How come our lives are so different?"

Around 4:00 P.M., Feng-yuan bought a bag of *dou-hua* (soft and semiliquid tofu) for Chun-lien, her three-year-old daughter, from a peddler. She told Chun-lien, "Take it home. Ask your father to help you." I was standing with four other women chatting in front of the sweatshop. Chun-lien came back a few minutes later with a bag of turbid *dou-hua*. Apparently, Chun-lien had dropped the bag somewhere on the way home. Feng-yuan got very upset. She yelled to Chun-lien, "Has your father died? What is this? If you didn't want to eat *dou-hua,* you shouldn't have asked for it. Now you've spoiled everything!" Feng-yuan grabbed the bag from Chun-lien and threw it into the garbage can. And yet she had not fully vented her frustration. She snatched a stick from the floor and started beating Chun-lien with it.

Women in the group began to say, "Maybe her father was sleeping." "Don't get so upset over such a trivial thing."

Chun-lien curled up on the ground screaming and crying. I went over and tried to take the stick away from Feng-yuan. One woman said, "That's enough. Don't beat Chun-lien any more. She is just a kid."

Feng-yuan dropped the stick and said, "You are women too. Can't you understand? I'm not just making pocket money!"

She went back to painting the stained glass. A woman came over to comfort Chun-lien. I took out a tissue to wipe Chun-lien's tears. A few seconds later, conversation had begun again on a different topic.

## "Smart Guys Should Avoid Standing Next to Me!"

In the satellite factory system, female members of the owners' families occupy a higher societal status than wage laborers, whether men or women. Even though they all participate in productive labor, the female members of the owner's family share whatever profit the factory makes, while the latter are rewarded only by daily wages. However, female family members lack power vis-à-vis male members of their families. In a sense, a woman does not really own her labor: it is under the control of the male household head and is appropriated by the family according to its needs. The dependence of female family members is enforced further by their unwaged status.

On the shop floor, the female family members often are assigned supervisory duties. Ching-may is a good example. She had worked in the factory ever since her husband, Mr. Li, started the business. I noticed that, during the time I stayed in this factory, she always took the key position in the production line to either set or speed up the pace. She also constantly gave orders to other workers. These observations are illustrated by the following excerpt from my field notes:

> Today I was assigned to wrap every wooden jewelry box with a piece of white paper. Show-Ii stood to my right putting each wrapped jewelry box into a colored paper box. Ching-may, the owner's wife, performed the next steps in the process by putting four styrofoam protectors on the bottom of each jewelry box, closing the bottom of the paper box, and then passing it to the next person, Ya-ling. Ya-ling in turn had to right the paper box, put another four protectors on the top of the jewelry box, and then close the cover of the paper box before passing it to the next person for final packing. Across the table, there were four workers doing the same job we were doing. I had to keep up the pace so that Show-Ii and the rest of the workers on my side would not be standing there without anything to do. Ching-may kept yelling to the workers who did the final packing to speed up. "Hey you, don't stand there. Hurry up!" she said. She yelled at San-mi, who stood across from me, "You are too slow. Go and switch with Jin-pao." San-mi went over to take Jin-pao's place to do the final packing. Jin-pao came and took over San-mi's job. Ching-may's yelling and giving orders were quite intimidating. While I was trying to push myself to go faster, I heard her say to Jin-pao, "Smart guys should avoid standing next to me. They get exhausted easily."

When female members of the factory-owning family monitor the labor process while participating in factory production, their labor becomes indispensable from the managerial point of view. Ching-may's husband told me that he had convinced Ching-may to take up the double burden of being a production worker and a cook in the factory. Every morning Ching-may went to the market at around 9:00. She joined other workers on the production line after coming back from the market, leaving to prepare lunch for the workers at around 11 o'clock. When she protested against the added burden, her husband told her,

> If you don't work in the factory as a worker, other workers are going to get lazy. You see, when you work, you work hard. A-meng [the supervisor's wife] would feel embarrassed if she doesn't work as hard as you. And the rest of the workers have to work hard when you set a standard like that.

Mr. Li proudly told me that he even told his wife that nothing comes free. In order to maintain the kind of lifestyle they currently enjoyed, such as owning a NT$940,000 (about US$36,000) American Pontiac, she had to assume the dual burden.

Because the female family members' role is clearly identified with the owner's interests, tension tends to build up on the shop floor between them and the female wage workers. In Wei-der, Yen-feng and her husband always aimed their frustration at their sister-in-law, the owner's wife. The daily exchanges on the shop floor were informative. The comments subtly reveal the conflict and tension between the two groups of women—those who are connected to the ownership of the means of production through marriages and those who are not.

> On July 10, 1989, Yen-feng's brother's son rushed back into the factory crying. He mumbled to his mother that I-chin, Yen-feng's daughter, had hit him. His mother comforted him by saying, "I am going to call the police to get her! I am going to call the police to get her." Yen-feng's husband was annoyed and asked the boy if he had hit I-chin first. The boy didn't answer. Across the working table, Yen-feng joined in: "He must have hit I-chin first. That's the way he is. I-chin would never hit anybody unless they touch her first." Yen-feng's sister-in-law kept saying that she was going to call the police to get I-chin. Apparently Yen-feng was upset by the false threats. She said to the boy, "If you two want to play together, you have to learn to get along with one another. Don't fight. If you want to fight, don't come to ask for help from your mother. You just have to fight it out between yourselves. It has nothing to do with the police, okay!" Yen-feng's sister-in-law became quiet after this.

One day, the truck came to collect the garbage. The practice in Taiwan involves taking the garbage to the truck that stops at the street corner. Yen-feng's sister-in-law asked I-chin to take the garbage out. I-chin's father said to the sister-in-law, "She is so young and you ask her to carry the garbage! What happens if the garbage spills all over the place? Why don't you ask your own son to do it?"

On another occasion, the conversation on the shop floor revealed both class conflict and familial tension. The older brother's son had gotten into an argument with I-chin. They had argued back and forth about whether the minivan belonged to the factory or to the boy's father. I-chin had insisted that the minivan belonged to the factory, and they had eventually come into the factory to resolve the argument.

> The boy said, "It has to be my father's." Yen-feng asked him why. "Otherwise, we don't have a car," the boy replied. His mother and father were smiling with pride on the other side of the working table.
>
> Yen-feng was annoyed. "We don't have a car either. If it's

your father's minivan and not the factory's, why don't you just wrap it up and bring it back to your living room tonight?" Yen-feng said.

Regarding the status and identity of the owners' wives in Taiwan's satellite factory system, several issues deserve further elaboration. First, my analysis of their indispensable roles is in accordance with Ka (1993) and Li and Ka's (1994) recent work on Taiwan's garment industry. In their studies, the owner's wife is characterized as "a general manager who is unwaged, multifunctional, an expert in production, with unconditional commitment, and never going to quit" (Ka 1993, 90). The nature of their involvement attests to the patriarchal and capitalist essence of the satellite factory system. Second, at the conceptual level, the owners' wives occupy a contradictory position that is derived from their affiliation with the petty capitalist class on the one hand and their status as unwaged workers on the other. This contradiction is associated with, and gives rise to, tension between their class and gender identities. Third, the pungent exchanges between an owner's wife and her relatives working in the factory as wage workers started off as fights between their children. After the adults were called upon to settle the fights, the trivial daily disputes were seized upon by the wage workers to lash out against the owner and his family. These incidents expose the gulf that divides the owners' wives and female wage workers who otherwise share identical gender interests. Thus I consider such verbal battles as episodes of class struggle. I will further elaborate the politics of verbal battles in Chapter 6 where I discuss the tactics of workers' resistance.

## Conclusions

Women's accounts of the first years of their marriage are invaluable for what they tell us about how a woman is molded into mother, wife, and daughter-in-law for her reproductive responsibilities, and into waged and/or unwaged worker for her productive responsibilities. The narratives depict a socialization process that documents the latest version of the patriarchal order in the Chinese family and shows the direct effects of capitalism on family organization. In the past, giving birth, especially to sons, was the customary way for newly married women to gain status in the family. As more and more married women participate into the labor force, becoming a mother means that one has to combine child-rearing with factory work. Adding one or more children to her family undermines the strength of whatever independence a married woman might gain through employment. Even when they have paid jobs, women with children are unlikely to leave an unfulfilling marriage because their wages are insufficient to support their children on their own. The possibility of remarriage is slim when there are children from a previous marriage.

The expansion into the factory system of women's labor within marriage illustrates how the coercive aspects of patriarchal power in the Chinese family are used for capitalist production. A recognition of the difficulties and struggles women have to go through adds an important dimension to our understanding of women's realities in the process of Taiwan's economic development.

Ethnographic data further show that women are fully aware of existing gender inequality and what it means to them in their daily lives. There is no distinction in *gender* identity between women married to factory owners and those whose husbands are workers. In contrast, these two groups of women are in direct conflict whenever class is at stake. The section "I'm Not Just Making Pocket Money" tells the story of a homeworker who was thrust into the position of a breadwinner. Her outcry testifies to the way in which labor of married women is conceptualized and institutionalized in the satellite factory system, whereas the significant role of the owners' wives in production and in labor control suggests that their class interest coincides with that of their husbands. Their unwaged status reinforces their dependence: only by identifying with their husbands in this way can they ensure their financial security. Consequently, their bond with other workers is relatively weak, or even nonexistent. One can therefore conclude that the gender consciousness of the owners' wives fails to transcend class boundaries, even though no one ever verbalized this issue to me explicitly in the course of my fieldwork. In this context, the spicy exchanges between the wives of owners and the female wage workers revealed how wage workers can expose and subtly assault the class affiliation of their boss's wife. The conflict along class lines took the form of daily disputes which, at first glance, can be easily dismissed as bearing no relevance to any overt labor politics on the shop floor. Furthermore, the owners' wives experience a real tension between their gender and their class identities. This manifests itself in their paradoxical relationship to the production system. While their nuptial ties to their husbands give them access to business profit, their labor is at the discretion of their husbands. Their indispensable contribution to the family business proves to be insufficient to alter the gender stratification. Therefore, the shared gender identity between the owners' wives and female wage workers needs to be viewed in the context of an "economic miracle" that exploits the patriarchal order in the name of economic development.

*Factory in the rice fields.*

*Craftmaster and apprentice cutting wooden boards in a box body factory.*

*Dusty wall of a box body factory.*

*A painting factory where wooden parts are painted and polished.*

*Hundreds of thousands of screws are made in this shack attached to an apartment building.*

*A typical scene in an assembly factory where various parts of wooden jewelry boxes are assembled, with children jumping up and down on the work table.*

*Outsiders assembling drawers in a box factory late at night.*

*The teenage son of an outsider removing rubber bands used to hold the newly glued drawers.*

*A homeworker painting stained glass at a neighborhood sweatshop, with her daughter's helping hands.*

*A child taking a nap on the shop floor of an assembly factory.*

*Owners' and workers' children in front of a living room–converted glass factory.*

*The kitchen of an assembly factory, with a sign on the wall stating that every worker has to wash his or her own rice bowl and that it is the duty of the owner's wife to do the dishes and final cleanup.*

*A local community center was lent to an electronic factory as a production site.*

*A matchmaker/factory worker posing with a groom's mother and sister prior to the engagement ceremony.*

# 5 The Everyday Construction of an Economic Miracle: Labor Control on the Shop Floor

$A$s a supplier of inexpensive manufactured goods in the world market, Taiwan has as its main concern the effective conversion of labor power into labor for its satellite factories. Technological innovation and upgrading, which are essential to increase productivity in craft-based production, are only marginally relevant in Taiwan's non-craft-based satellite factory system. From the owners' viewpoint, profit is primarily correlated with the productivity level of the workers. The level of labor control is intensified because many Taiwanese manufacturers are involved in seasonal trade. There is a clear distinction between the slack season and the peak season for factories producing Christmas ornaments and gifts. In the peak season, temporary workers are recruited, working hours are extended, and productivity per person and time unit is driven to the maximum. Oppressive labor practices and rigid labor controls are especially severe. Both the factories and the workers are managed under the assumption that they must earn a whole year's living within a half-year period.

The constraint of seasonal trading is especially prominent in the satellite factories. These firms are less likely to diversify to other lines of production in the slack season because of the fragmentation of production and limited investment. Among the six factories in which I was a participant observer in the summer of 1989, one factory completely closed down in the winter of 1989 because of the lack of work orders. The other five factories made cuts in their labor force, the cuts ranging from one-third to one-half. The working schedule also adjusted to this slowdown. Workers had every Sunday and every Saturday afternoon off. They also took off around 5:30 in the afternoon for the rest of the week, instead of at 9 o'clock in the evening. The workers were paid only for the time they actually worked in the factories. That is, during the slack season, workers were no longer given opportunities to sell their labor.

Pressures induced by seasonal trading have become more prominent in recent years. Fluctuation in foreign exchange rates has made foreign buyers shorten the period of time between placing an order and the final delivery date in order to minimize risk.[1] Taiwan's local producers are now even less able to predict what will happen in the next peak season, and workers have lost what little control they had over the way in which their labor is appropriated in the satellite factories.

Married women who work as insiders in the satellite factories are treated as *"married female* workers." The assumption is that they can afford to be laid off or paid substantially less during the slack season because they are supported by the family breadwinner, rather than being the breadwinner themselves. During the peak season, however, married women are no longer treated as *"married female* workers" with family responsibilities to fulfill. Whenever the factories need them, they are forced to sell their labor on the same terms as other workers and are penalized if they fail to make themselves fully available. On the one hand, the system makes it extremely difficult for married women who work as insiders to fulfill their family responsibilities during the peak season. On the other hand, the factories use their marital status to deprive married women of their right to be treated as regular workers who have to make a living even in the slack season.

Even though most workers in the satellite factories are related to the owners either as relatives, neighbors, or direct family members, their interests are not identical with those of the owners, as they do not share the same socioeconomic position. Generally speaking, there are at least two groups of workers in the satellite factories: members of the owner's immediate family who work in the factories as either unpaid or waged laborers, and non–family members who work for wages. On the shop floor, increases of productivity are realized predominantly through rigorous control of the latter by the former.

## Means of Labor Control

In order to convert a maximum amount of the workers' labor power into labor, multiple schemes of labor control are employed. Here I examine how work schedules, wage systems, and boarding arrangements are used to increase productivity.

In contrast to large factories with two or three shifts, the satellite factories work one shift with long hours. The following is a typical peak-season working schedule for the insiders in a satellite factory.[2]

| Monday | 8:00 A.M.–12:00 noon, 1:00 P.M.–5:00 P.M., 5:30 P.M.–9:00 P.M. |
|---|---|
| Tuesday | 8:00 A.M.–12:00 noon, 1:00 P.M.–5:00 P.M., 5:30 P.M.–9:00 P.M. |
| Wednesday | 8:00 A.M.–12:00 noon, 1:00 P.M.–6:00 P.M. |
| Thursday | 8:00 A.M.–12:00 noon, 1:00 P.M.–5:00 P.M., 5:30 P.M.–9:00 P.M. |
| Friday | 8:00 A.M.–12:00 noon, 1:00 P.M.–5:00 P.M., 5:30 P.M.–9:00 P.M. |
| Saturday | 8:00 A.M.–12:00 noon, 1:00 P.M.–6:00 P.M. |
| Sunday | 8:00 A.M.–12:00 noon, 1:00 P.M.–6:00 P.M. (every other week) |

Workers are expected to sell their labor no fewer than twenty-eight days a month, for from nine to eleven and a half hours a day. On Monday, Tuesday, Thursday, and Friday, they get one hour off for lunch and thirty minutes off for supper. On Wednesday, Saturday, and Sunday, they work until six o'clock in the evening. Lunch and supper are usually prepared by the owner's wife within the factory. Some factories provide the meal free, as part of the benefit package. Others deduct a fixed amount for food from the workers' wages. The latter practice always creates tension, since the workers may not get the kind of meal they pay for. Some workers go home to have their meal, usually those who live nearby and, therefore, can make it back on time. For example, Ms. Tsai lives next door to the factory. Her mother, a widow, stays with her and does the cooking. Ms. Chang lives in a traditional peasant housing complex five minutes from the factory. Her husband, a farmer, does the cooking.

The evening hours are considered overtime. Although the general understanding is that, during the peak season, insiders have to work four evenings per week, workers often are asked to put in more hours to meet deadlines. Or, they may get a Tuesday evening off unexpectedly. The overtime schedule is announced on a daily basis. Some factories put up a sign next to the time clock announcing either *jiaban* (overtime) or *bujiaban* (no overtime). The workers learn whether or not they will have to work overtime when they punch in that day. Other factories announce the overtime around three o'clock in the afternoon. On Wednesday, Saturday, and Sunday, such an announcement usually causes some unfriendly, even hostile, reactions from the floor. As factory work is physically demanding, such sentiments tend to be especially strong if the workers have been overworked for quite a while, say with no break for more than a week.

Evening overtime frequently lasts past nine o'clock, and employees usually do not know how late they will have to work. The hours are controlled by the owner according to the deadline for each order.[3] In one assembly factory where I worked, we were once asked to finish an order of 1,700 wooden jewelry boxes before the night ended. We were so tired that the shop floor became very quiet, no conversation, only sounds from the machine and shifting the boxes. Our hands continued the repetitive moves. Everyone looked very pale with no facial expression whatsoever. Around 11:00, the owner's wife asked the overseer to ask the owner if we could quit for the day and restart in the morning. The overseer went upstairs to ask Mr. Li. He came back announcing, "Continue until the whole thing gets done." No one seemed to be moved by the announcement. We continued to drag our bodies along to perform the task we were asked to perform. Around 12:30 Mr. Li came downstairs. He asked the overseer to count the cardboard boxes to see how many pieces were left to be finished. "About five hundred," said the overseer. Mr. Li said, "Okay, let's quit for tonight. We will restart tomorrow." Mr. Li told me the next day, "Sometimes it's important to push it. The old Chinese proverb says, 'It is better to brace oneself for a challenge in the first attempt rather than to try it again and again.' Sometimes I have to push them way beyond the limit, rather than letting the morale go and having to pick it up again later on."

When I asked about their schedule, the workers always mentioned the terms *da libai* (big weekend) and *xiao libai* (small weekend). During the *da libai,* the second and fourth weekends of every month, the workers are supposed to have Sunday off. During the *xiao libai,* they have to work. This may not always be the case, since the owner usually makes the work schedule fit the deadlines. The workers may be asked to work three consecutive weeks on an order, with no day off, and then get one Thursday off after the order has been completed.

The same work schedule applied in almost all of the satellite factories I visited. The exception was a hinge factory where the owner was an alcoholic. The owner of the hardware factory that does business with this hinge factory always complained about it:

Some of them are really backward. They don't care about their business. They are like the old-fashioned peasant. Get up and work at sunrise. Go back and rest at sunset. As long as they make enough money, they seldom work overtime. It is extremely frustrating to do business with these old-fashioned craftsmen. You have to beg them when you are really under deadline pressure. I sometimes have to bring wine with me when I ask him to work overtime for me.

In the course of my fieldwork research in the factories, I got extremely exhausted. Sometimes I fell asleep when I tried to finish my field notes at night. Twice I went to work unaware of the fact that I had put my T-shirt on inside out. When I asked the workers how they could work so hard, some told me, "After a while, you get used to it." They talked about their schedule as if it were the normal pattern of working life. However, my observation did not convince me that this was the case. The husband of a sixty-year-old female worker complained that his wife looked as if she was about to "drop dead" when she got back home in the evening. My married coworkers realized that others "have better luck in life. They only work five and half days every week." A married woman with two children summarized her experiences as an insider thus: "We either don't have enough time to earn the money out there. Or, we have plenty of time and there is no money to earn."

The wage system is another means of labor control. Because insiders are paid by the day, how much one earns is closely tied to how well one can fit in with the factory schedule. The system is designed to ensure that every worker will be on the job no less than twenty-eight days a month in the peak season. The potential monthly income is composed of four parts: wages for the four Sundays, wages for the two Sundays of *xiao libai,* twenty-six days of regular wages, and bonuses for full attendance. The pay for the four Sundays is regarded as "free money" by both owners and workers. The owners feel they are paying for the two Sundays not worked, and are paying overtime for the other two. For their part, the workers cannot see how people like themselves can get paid without doing at least nine hours of sweaty work. The concept of "free money" is therefore employed to regulate workers' attendance.

Absenteeism is discouraged by offering a bonus to workers who take off only the factory-designated holidays. The amount of these attendance bonuses ranges from NT$600 to NT$1,200. There are two ways to calculate the bonuses. Some factories use a half month as the unit, others the whole month. The workers told me that they prefer the half-month system because, with this basis of calculation, even if someone takes a day off at the beginning of a month, it is still possible for him/her to receive 50 percent of the bonus if he/she does not take any day off in the second half of the month.[4]

Besides, if a worker joins the factory on the 15th, he/she loses the four days off with pay of that month, plus the attendance bonuses. In order to illustrate how take-home pay is affected by various rules used to calculate monthly income, the following is a hypothetical calculation of the different wages received by someone who works twenty-seven days a month instead of twenty-eight. With a daily rate of NT$280, calculation A shows a worker who receives two Sundays off with pay, two Sundays with pay plus wages for overtime, wages for 26 regular days, and the $600 full attendance bonus. Calculation B shows the amount the same worker would receive if he/she took a regular working day off. A decrease of $860 results from the loss of $280 for one Sunday of the "free money," $280 for the day not worked, and $300 for the full attendance bonuses. Calculation C shows what happens if the worker is absent on one of the two working Sundays: he/she loses two days of "free money," that day's wages, and $300 of the full attendance bonus.

A.   $280 × 2 + $280 × (2+2) + $280 × 26 + $300 + $300 = $9,560
B.   $280 × 1 + $280 × (2+2) + $280 × 25 + $300 = $8,700
C.   $280 × 1 + $280 × (1 + 1) + $280 × 26 + $300 = $8,420

From calculation B we see that even though workers are allowed two Sundays off with pay, they lose this privilege if they do not work the full 28 days a month.

A comparison of the principles underlying the way workers' wages are calculated and those that inform the organization of their working schedule shows a contradiction between these two. The working schedule is designed to give the owner absolute flexibility: the workers get four days off with pay each month, regardless of which four days. The wage system, in contrast, is totally inflexible: it penalizes workers who, instead of following the schedule decided by the owner, actually arrange the break on their own. If the idea is that the workers should get four days off with pay regardless of which four days, they should not be asked to give up the "free money" when they take a regular working day off. The decrease in monthly wages should result only from the loss of the daily wage for that specific day, and of the attendance bonus. Following the same logic, workers should not be asked to give up either the attendance bonus or the "free money" when they decide not to go to work on the two "working" Sundays, providing they have put in the full twenty-eight working days for that month. Calculations D and E show how much a worker would have received, had his/her wages been paid consistently with the way the working schedule is organized:

D.   $280 × 2 + $280 × (2+2) + $280 × 25 + $300 = $8,980
E.   $280 × 2 + $280 × (1+2) + $280 × 26 + $300 + $300 = $9,280

In D, the worker takes a weekday off. In E, the worker decides not to go to work on one of the "working Sundays." There is a big difference between these calculations and the ones actually implemented by the factory, as shown in B and C. The existence of such contradictions suggests that the owners use the wage system and the work schedule together for the purposes of labor control and capital accumulation.

The peculiar wage system and work schedules customary in the satellite factories violate the workers' rights granted by the Standard Labor Law. Overtime payment practices in the satellite system also contravene state regulations. Overtime pay for evening work is calculated according to the workers' daily wages. Depending on the factory, they get half a day's pay (four hours) for each three or three and a half hours they put in after five o'clock on weekdays. That is to say, the workers earn between 14 percent and 33 percent more for overtime. This increase does not apply to the two Sundays, since the "free money" payment has effectively doubled the wage already.

The workers are further constrained by the way paydays are scheduled. In the satellite factories, the workers do not receive their pay on the first of every month. Instead, they have to wait until the fifth. This unusual arrangement affects workers who want to quit one factory and start a new job at another. In order to leave with wages from the previous month in hand, they have to put in another five days of work. If, later on, they want to get the wages for these five working days, they need to come back to their former workplace the following month. They have to take a day off and lose wages at the new job. According to one bookkeeper, workers seldom come back to get the five days of wages owing, especially if their new job is in another city. As a result, when workers change jobs, they lose a substantial amount of income. Not only do they lose the five days of wages due from their previous employer; they also lose the chance to receive the first month's "free money," attendance bonuses, and regular wages for days missed from their new job. The manner of calculation and the payday schedule together ensure that an owner gets five working days of free labor from every worker who leaves his factory. This practice also structurally suppresses the turnover rate.

Because of the heavy workload and the low wages, most workers do not feel they can afford to take a day off. However, on the day right after payday, an urge to relax and enjoy the fruits of one's hard work becomes especially strong. With their wages in hand, girls want to buy something for their parents or themselves. Boys feel they can afford at least one visit to the prostitutes. Married women want to get some snacks or supplies for their children. Married men want to get together with friends to have a drink. The relaxed atmosphere starts one or two days before payday. Some workers talk across the worktable about what they plan to do with their money. Others talk about what they did the first time they were paid. Still others recall happy memories or moments in the past when there was a major purchase. After talking about, and listening to, the plans and memories, it becomes psychologically difficult for the workers not to take one or two days off after payday. Every month absenteeism reaches its height during this time, as the young single men go to prostitutes, and the young single women either visit their boyfriends who are working in the same city or return home. Married couples may take a trip to their in-laws' house. In some cases, this is the only time working parents get to see their children who have been left behind or sent away.[5]

Several factories that I observed took absenteeism into consideration when they organized the work orders. Usually, the deadlines for large orders were arranged to be finished just before payday. Such an arrangement not only minimizes the effects of absenteeism; but by increasing the likelihood that the workers will take days off because of exhaustion, it also decreases the amount of full-attendance bonuses the owner has to pay. In all my time in the factories, the owners never called a day off right after payday. It remained the workers' own choice to stay away from work and so to forgo the NT$300 bonus.

Although there are differences among the factories and among workers, it is possible to tabulate the overall discrepancy between the daily practices in the satellite factories and relevant regulations of the Standard Labor Law (see Table 5.1). Although the owners never hesitate to portray the job opportunities they provide as a big favor to the workers, the system is oppressive in nature and, in many cases, violates the workers' rights granted by the law.

TABLE 5.1

Differences between Labor Practices and Labor Law

| | Labor Practices[a] | Labor Law[b] |
|---|---|---|
| Workload per week | 11.5 hours for 4 days and 8.5 hours for 3 days | 8 hours for 6 days |
| Overtime | One day off every other week Arbitrary; decided by the owner | One day off every week Agreed upon by the workers or union; state notification and approval required |
| No limit | A maximum of 4 hours per day and 46 hours per month for males and 32 hours for females | Special state approval required |
| Overtime pay | 14.4% to 33% increase with no difference in hours for the weekdays | 33% increase for the first 2 hours and 66.6% increase for 2 to 4 hours |
| | No overtime increase for Sundays or holidays | 100% increase for Sundays and holidays |
| | Workers lose full attendance bonuses when they do not work overtime | Workers should not be penalized if they do not work overtime |
| Wages | Daily wages with two days off per month (28 days work, 30 days pay) | Daily wages with four days off per month (26 days work, 30 days pay) |
| | Large percentage of workers are paid below the standard wages | Workers' wages should not be lower than the standard wages decided by the state |
| Vacation | No vacation | Vacation with pay |

SOURCES: [a]Generated from my field notes.
[b]Laogong Xingzheng Zazhishe (1989).

Owners use several other techniques to cut production costs and further expand control over the workers' daily lives. Providing room and board for the workers is a common practice. Workers who live thirty minutes or more away from the factories usually stay at the factory, especially during the peak season. The room are generally located upstairs or next-door to the factory. They are small, stuffy, and extremely hot and humid in the summer. Every morning the workers have to get ready early enough not to miss their breakfast. After lunch, they take a fifteen- to twenty-minute nap and are awakened by the owner five minutes before the work starts up again. The following example illustrates how living arrangements and time management are used together for labor control.

> A-tong, a deliverer for the assembly factory Ta-you, rents a room with his girlfriend in an apartment building three blocks from the factory. One morning the owner warned him, "Lately, I have noticed that you don't get here on time. Sometimes, you even get here three minutes after eight o'clock. Although you don't live in the factory, you should still get here at least five minutes before eight so that I don't need to run around finding you."

The workers who stay in the factory dormitory also lose the freedom to take a day off because of the interior organization of the factories. For example, in a shabby, temporarily constructed factory, the dormitory and the main office are both upstairs, while the bathroom, kitchen, and the factory production line are downstairs. Unless the worker leaves the dormitory and the factory altogether, the physical environment can be anxiety provoking. The workers who stay in the dormitory cannot even go to the bathroom without being seen by coworkers and possibly approached by the owner. In one incident Gwei-may, a young female worker, decided to take a day off on the first day of her period, but she acted as if she had done something shameful. When Gwei-may's close friend brought water and her own lunch to share with Gwei-may around 12:30, Gwei-may asked the friend, "Where is the owner's wife? Is now a good time for me to go to the bathroom?"

For married couples, living in the factory dormitory implies sacrifices. They are lucky if they get their own room. In some cases, the wife and children stay in one room with other female workers, while the husband is separately housed with the male workers. The meals are poor in quality and meager in quantity. Children who stay with their parents in the factory do not receive meal allotments. Adding children to the table means that everyone else has less to eat. Because of the limited quantity of the daily meal, compromises and sacrifices have to be made. Mothers with children are very conscious of this aspect of their daily lives. At the table, they make an effort to curb their children's appetites. This task is not easy because of the lack of meat in their daily diet. The mothers always mix the rice with gravy from the dishes for their children as another way of restraining their appetites. In one factory, mothers with children took turns washing everybody's dishes after the meals, to compensate their coworkers for their tolerance and sacrifices. Although this particular incident has little to do with labor control per se, it tells a great deal about how Taiwan's "economic miracle" is constructed in a local and daily way.

## Surveillance on the Shop Floor

The oppressive labor practices that I have described are combined with close surveillance on the shop floor. The surveillance is carried out in two forms: personal surveillance and the putting-out system. The way supervision is carried out is unique to the satellite factory system.

One aspect of this system is that many owners and, often, their family members, work in the factory themselves. Usually it is hard to recognize the owner from his appearance. For example, Mr. Cheng, the owner of a wooden box body factory, usually wore a dark gray shirt and old black pants and was barefoot like the other two male workers in the factory. I was not able to tell who the owner was when I first visited the factory. Many of the owners claim that there is really no difference between them and their employees, since they do exactly the same kind of work that their employees are asked to perform. They proudly told me that they themselves were former workers. According to them, the workers should not complain because as long as they work hard, one day they too will "make it."

After working in several factories myself, however, I came to understand why many owners continue to work on the shop floor even when their labor is no longer strictly necessary. The most obvious reason is that, by working among the workers, the owner sets a pace with which the rest of the workers must keep up. Ms. Chang, a female worker in her early sixties, described to me how exhausting it was to work with the owner, Mr. Cheng.

> When he wants to get the work done, he runs like a crazy dog. You should see him. I have never seen a guy work as hard as that! I always scold him. I ask him if he is about to die or what. Otherwise, why rush like a crazy dog.

By being present on the shop floor, the owners are able to supervise and monitor the labor process closely. They catch any mismanagement on the spot and prevent potential waste in material as well as human resources. Here is an example where the workers' labor was maximized under the supervision of the owner:

> It was about 2:30 in the afternoon when I joined the workers. I counted the number of the workers who were currently working on the second table. There were eighteen, including the owner, Mr. Li. The work was divided into several steps. It started with putting the glass on the door, followed by wiping the mirror, blowing the wooden box clean, checking the music device, inspecting the body of the box, wrapping the white paper, putting the wooden box into the colored paper box, and putting six paper boxes in a large cardboard box. Workers were standing one next to another to do whatever they were asked to do. Because not enough jewelry boxes were ready for packing, Mr. Li started to reorganize the workforce after around 3:00. He told some of the workers to move to the first table where another model was being assembled. The number of workers at the second table decreased to eleven around 3:00, five around 3:15, three around 3:20. All the workers were told to move to the first table around 3:25.

As the owner of an assembly factory pointed out to me, it is easier to make a profit by having many small factories produce various parts for him because "you then get many owners who will watch their own workers closely."

## The Putting-Out System

In addition to such direct supervision and monitoring, the owners also structure the production process on the assembly line for the purpose of labor control. For example, in the wooden jewelry boxes factories described in Chapter 3, both outsiders and insiders worked side by side to carry out the production work. The difference is that the outsiders, who usually specialize in tasks such as screwing the hanger, door, and handles to the wooden jewelry boxes or gluing the interior flannel into the boxes, were hired by the subcontractor who got contracts from more than one factory, while the insiders were hired by the factory owner. Because the outsiders are hired for a fixed quantity of work on a piece-rate basis, the sooner they finish the work, the earlier they can take on a new contract in another factory. It is in the subcontractor's interest to shorten the amount of time they spend on each contract. However, this is not the case for the insiders, who are paid daily wages and, therefore, do not have the incentive to speed up. The following represents a typical arrangement.

I. Outsiders     II. Insiders     III. Outsiders     IV. Insiders

By alternating groups of outsiders and insiders, the owners pressure the insiders to keep up with the pace set by the outsiders who precede them on the line. If the insiders fail to do so, the failure stands out right away, since the unfinished products begin to pile up in the space between the groups. The insiders are also pressured to perform by the outsiders who are next on the line because unless the productivity is compatible with that of these outsiders, the latter will be idle because of lack of work. Therefore, it is in the direct interest of the subcontractor of outsiders to make sure that the insiders comply with the structural control. The following excerpt from my field notes shows how the tension built up in one such assembly line:

> The two insiders talk to one another while they are sticking the mirror into the wooden boxes. This conversation apparently holds down the speed and affects the rest of the workers on the assembly line. Three outsiders sit next to them to screw on the hanger and doors after the mirror gets put into the boxes. The outsiders frequently stop and wait as the two insiders' conversation gets longer and longer. Finally, the contractor loses his patience. He simply yells at the two insiders, "Hey, we have been waiting for you. . . . It doesn't matter how hard you work. We are different. Don't you know that?" This outburst stops the two insiders' chat. After the speed picks up for a while, the contractor then yells at the insiders to his right, "Why don't you speed up? Can't you see the boxes are piling up here?"

## The Social Construction of Paternalism

The underlying mechanism that connects the multiple schemes of labor control and various oppressive labor practices is the construction of paternalism. The term *paternalism* does not always have the same meaning. Bookman (1988) uses it to describe a close, personal, and arbitrary style of labor control. The focus is on a specific style of management. Others have used *paternalism* to emphasize the organizational aspects of the factory. For example, Cole (1971) employs the term to describe the characteristics of the typical Japanese factory. He shows that Japanese employers create and foster family-like characteristics to blur potential conflicts of interest in the workplace. Dublin (1979) describes the situation in nineteenth-century Lowell, Massachusetts, as paternalistic because young single female workers were under close supervision in the dormitory where simulated familial discipline was imposed. Burawoy (1985) uses *paternalism* to describe what happened when male heads of families gradually lost their autonomy to factory owners in nineteenth-century Lancashire, England. As Burawoy puts it, the factory regime became paternalistic because it was "government *through* the family," as opposed to the patriarchal factory regime where "government *by* the family" was the norm (1985, 98).

The term *paternalism* describes well the power structure in Taiwan's satellite manufacturing system.[6] The various forms of control are enforced by the daily construction of paternalism based on a preexisting family system and kinship structure. Because many owners hire relatives, the conflict of interest between the factory owner and the waged workers often take the form of familial disagreement. The construction of paternalism is a product of a constant struggle between those who own the means of production and those who sell their labor in the satellite factories.

Because the work involved in the satellite factories is mainly unskilled and labor intensive, capital accumulation is dependent upon how much of the workers' labor power is converted into labor. How to get a heterogeneous group to accept the oppressive labor practices day after day is a major concern for the owner. A hidden dimension of Taiwan's economic miracle, the everyday construction of paternalism in Taiwan's satellite factories, serves to sustain oppressive labor practices in the interests of the factory owners.

### *Ethnicity and the Social Construction of Paternalism*

Generally speaking, Taiwanese paternalism is based on the ethnic and the kinship systems. Let us take the example of Ta-you, a satellite factory that assembles parts into wooden jewelry boxes. Ta-you maintains a labor force of thirty workers during the peak season. The majority of the workers are indigenous and have come from remote mountain areas. Mr. Li, an indigene himself, is known to be good at managerial tactics. Once he told me proudly how he boosted productivity by informing the workers that it is in their best interest to work hard.

> I need to know what to tell them to boost productivity. Usually I tell them that it is not easy for an indigene to own a factory in the city. In order to survive, every one of us has to work extra hard. If you don't work hard, the factory may become bankrupt. When that happens, I'll still be able to live idly for at least three years. How about you? You may end up being nowhere. I doubt that you would ever be able to find another job in the city.

Even though it is not really true that the workers will not be able to find other jobs, Mr. Li still used this threat to motivate his workers. In some instances he deliberately created a paternalistic context to discipline the workers. At other times, he introduced ethnic pride to strengthen his statements. On one occasion, two days after the workers received their wages, Chung-ming, a 15-year-old male worker, was asked to see Mr. Li in the office. It seems that Chung-ming had gone out with two other young male workers the night they got paid, and they had not come back until that morning. The following is what Mr. Li told Chung-ming in the office:

> You simply disappeared for all this time. . . . If you had asked me, I would have given you my permission. If you had asked me ten times [for a day off], I'd have given you eleven. . . . You should at least let me or your uncle [who worked in the same factory] know before you do anything like this [take a day off]. . . . Those two other kids went with you. They didn't come back until you did. . . . Hey! Look at me when I talk to you. Don't look somewhere else.
>     Your freedom has interfered with others' freedom, you know. . . . You are my relative, aren't you? Would you say that you are not my relative? I consider everybody who comes from Sheng-cheng [the village where Mr. Li and many other workers come from] as my relatives. . . . When you take a day off, you lose your salary. This also affects the factory's productivity. It may be all right with you, since you don't have a family to support. Others are different. Those kids have to give their money to their parents. I don't think they would have taken the day off if it weren't for you. Ta-you is different from other factories. We are better. We are all indigenous. If you don't work hard, I will not consider you as indigene. You wouldn't deserve it. You would just be one of them, the Han people. . . . You should not become a person who takes a lead in fooling around. . . . Ta-you can't survive without you, you know. Considering your age, you can call me father. My son, Kwang Li, is the same age as you. . . . As long as you work hard, I will give you permission to take off. In case you don't have enough money for fun, I can even lend you some.

Kwei-may, a 14-year-old female indigenous worker, came to work in Ta-you one month before me. She told me that she missed her mother very much, "but they don't let me go home." Her family lived in a remote village in the mountains. It took her about six hours to go home by bus. She had to transfer in Pu-li, a town two hours from her village, from where only two buses go to her village each day. Visiting home was therefore a long trip for Kwei-may. One day Kwei-may told me that she planned to visit home after getting that month's pay. She wanted to get some medicine and daily supplies for her mother who had been sick for a while. However, I saw Kwei-may continue working in the factory after payday. She looked very pale and hardly talked to anyone. When I finally got a chance to speak to her several days later, she told me that the Mr. Li had not allowed her to take the days off. She was told to wait for another month.

### Kinship and the Social Construction of Paternalism

Other factory owners have always attributed Ta-you's high productivity to Mr. Li's skillful manipulation of the indigenous people by appealing to their ethnic pride. Its success, however, also owed much to the control Mr. Li was able to exert through the familial/kinship system. To illustrate the latter approach, it is fruitful to look at another assembly factory, Wei-der, which was clearly organized upon a preexisting kinship system. In 1989, Wei-der was jointly owned by the older brother of Yen-feng (a female worker at Wei-der), and her second and third uncles. Because the second uncle ran a seafood restaurant, he only contributed capital. It was the third uncle and Yen-feng's older brother, along with their immediate families, who were directly involved in the management and production of Wei-der. The third uncle oversaw the contracting of labor, and Yen-feng's older brother managed the factory. In addition to the outside piece-rate workers supplied by subcontractors, Wei-der had eight wage workers: Yen-feng's husband, aunt (the third uncle's wife), sister-in-law (the older brother's wife), three cousins (three children of the third uncle), Showcheng (a woman outside the family), and Yen-feng herself. In the peak summer season, Yen-feng's older sister came to cook for the factory so that the sister-in-law could be freed for production work.

Yen-feng had been married for about eight years. Her seven-year-old son stayed with her mother-in-law in Tao-Yuan, about a three hours' drive away from Wei-der. A three-year-old daughter, I-chin, lived with Yen-feng and her husband at the factory.

Before getting married, Yen-feng had worked in a shoe factory. After her marriage, she quit her job and moved into her in-laws' household in the northern part of Taiwan. Yen-feng's husband, Jeng-zi, came to work in Wei-der because he had injured his knees three years before and it was better for him to live in the central part of Taiwan where the weather is less humid. Yen-feng and her daughter had joined her husband the previous year. Like others, Yen-feng and her husband were paid on a daily basis, but her husband received a higher rate.

Under customary law, Yen-feng, as a woman, was not entitled to inherit property from her father. Her older brother used his inheritance to start Wei-der with the two uncles. Yen-feng and her husband were thus excluded from sharing in the profits made by the factory. They received only wages, and did not even share in the bonuses given to the uncles and her older brother. Yen-feng and Jeng-zi therefore had little incentive to work as hard as, say, the wives of Yen-feng's brother and uncles.

Many problems in Wei-der were handled as familial matters, even though they involved a conflict of interest between those who owned the means of production and those who sold their labor. For example, one Wednesday afternoon, Yen-feng's sister-in-law announced that everybody had to work that evening in order to meet the deadline.

> Yen-feng got very upset. She had just told me that they had not had any days or nights off since last Monday. As soon as she heard the announcement, she protested, "I thought we could have at least three nights off every week." Yen-feng's husband, who was working across the table, joined the protest, "Hey, we are being mistreated. This isn't right!" The sister-in-law put on an apologetic smile. "You have to talk to your older brother. This is not my decision."

Asking them to talk to the "older brother" simply transformed the conflict of interest between classes into a disagreement within the family. It also justified the legitimacy of that decision, since, in the context of the Chinese family, the older brother has full authority to settle any familial dispute in the absence of the father. The discontent died out. I was told the next day that they worked until ten o'clock that evening.

Kinship relationships are not only used by the owners to their own advantage; they are also sometimes relied upon by the workers in fighting back. For example, in Wei-der, one afternoon, there was a problem with some paper boxes that were too small to fit the wooden jewelry boxes. As the temperature in the factory went up, everybody on the shop floor got more and more impatient with the problem. Yen-feng finally yelled at her daughter, "Go get your uncle!" Thus, instead of approaching her brother (the manager) herself, Yen-feng asked a third party, her three-year-old daughter, to initiate the complaint. In addition, I-chin was asked to "get the uncle." Once again, a purely technical/production problem was transformed into a familial issue. In other words, the brother was called in not as a manager but as a family member who was expected to be responsible for the well-being of others in the family.

## Conclusions

The many schemes of labor control employed by the bosses in their effort to maximize labor productivity pose a vivid contrast with the various adjustments made by married women as they seek to carry out their reproductive function. Taken together, Chapters 4 and 5 illustrate how Taiwan's economic miracle has largely been created by the labor of married women. The satellite manufacturing system is closely intertwined with preexisting family and kinship systems. Nevertheless, the heterogenous nature of the labor force within the satellite system makes conflict between bosses and workers a constant feature of daily life. In the next chapter, I discuss labor politics and workers' resistance in the satellite factory in greater detail, from the women's perspective.

# 6

# Are Women Really "Petty Minded"? Awareness, Compliance, and Resistance in the Workplace

Owners make every effort to establish social ties with their employees in order to disguise the materialistic aspects of employment. In defiance of the oppressive labor practices to which they are subject, the workers, for their part, employ tactics that are informal, individualized, and clandestine. None of their struggles aim to challenge the satellite factory system as such. Nor do they take an organized and confrontational form. Just the same, the workers' actions to mitigate excessive claims on their labor reveal a systematic pattern.

## Issues of Labor Subordination: Awareness, Compliance, and Resistance

Studies of labor politics typically focus on organized, collective, and confrontational actions. Viewed from this perspective, the labor movements in Asia's newly industrializing countries have been singularly weak and ineffective. Scholars seeking to explain this weakness either attribute it to the passivity of female workers (F.-S. Huang, 1977) or account for it by pointing to single factors, whether ideological, political, or economic. Other studies have proposed a structural explanation that stresses the social and economic context within which these factors operate (Deyo 1987, 1989). There is also some indication that patriarchal power has impeded workers' unionizing activities in Taiwan. Chang (1990) shows that, in a recent strike, the participation of married female garment workers in union activities was blocked by their husbands. Hsia (1990) finds that employers strategically put pressure on the parents and relatives of both male and female union activists, and labor-management confrontation is eventually palliated by "pressures from the family members and relatives" (Hsia 1990, 133).

Studies of socioeconomically disadvantaged groups have noted a variety of acts of resistance that do not fit the definition of a large-scale labor movement. In Malaysia production was interrupted in multinational corporations when the female workers claimed that they were possessed by religious spirits (Ong 1987). Poor peasants in Malaysia employ petty pilfering, malicious gossip, and livestock murdering to clothe their resistance (Scott 1985). Female immigrant workers in Silicon Valley have been shown to play gender- or race-based stereotypes off against the management's effort to increase productivity (Hossfeld 1990).

It must be remembered that there are no legal grounds upon which unions can be organized in Taiwan's satellite factories. Therefore, large-scale collective confrontations are ruled out. Resistance must assume the form of individual struggle on the shop floor. Various tactics are developed by the workers either to resist unwarranted labor appropriation or to ensure fair play. These tactics are defensive in nature. In most cases, workers direct their protest against the individual owner. Because workers in the satellite factory system are divided into insiders, outsiders, and homeworkers, institutionalized tension exists between these groups. As a result of these constraints, the owners' and workers' awareness of labor subordination, the workers' compliance, and the forms of worker resistance can most appropriately be analyzed in the context of the social relationships that are constructed both by the owners and the workers.

## The Social Context of Resistance

In Taiwan's satellite factories, both owners and workers strive to add a personal dimension to the formal relations based on employment, so that they may call upon it for their own purposes. Because they regard their labor as so valuable that it cannot be entirely compensated for by wages, the workers expect something nonmonetary from the owners in return for the opportunity to utilize that labor. The implicit expectations include higher wages, job security, and accommodations for child-rearing responsibilities—the kinds of things that they cannot secure through formal labor legislation. The owner, most often a male, often goes out of his way to make sure that his workers are indebted to him personally. When the owner demands something from the worker, he constructs the demand as if he is simply reclaiming a personal debt.

I thus pierce through the disguising curtain of "personal" and "informal" owner-worker relationships in small-scale family-centered enterprises. This approach asks how such informality is negotiated, achieved, and maintained on a daily basis; what is the practical function of such arrangements; and what can we learn from them about the overall labor politics of the satellite factory system. Doing so enables me to show that the seemingly informal and personalized labor-management relationships in fact entail continual, calculated effort from both workers and owners in their struggle for an acceptable working relationship. I therefore have a problem with descriptions of these relationships such as that presented by Stites. In his discussion of why married women find neighborhood factories attractive, Stites reports:

> They can chat with coworkers, who are often neighbors, and keep an eye on small children who may occasionally be brought to work with them. No one gets particularly upset if they miss a day of work or arrive late due to personal business. (Stites 1982, 259)

Such accounts mistakenly imply that the workers do not feel any sense of social obligation in the informal work relationship. These accounts fail to recognize that the concept of mutual obligation constitutes an important, though unwritten, aspect of the owner-worker relationship in Taiwan's satellite system, as well as playing a significant role in the daily politics of labor within the factory. In this section I employ ethnographic data to illustrate the personal dimension of the owner-worker relationship as a construct in which both parties have a great deal invested.

### "We Came to Help"

The concept of "help" (*bangmang* or *bang*) is widely used among workers in the satellite factories, in a variety of contexts. On some occasions, workers use the term to disguise their employment status. For example, quite often a worker substitutes "employed by [somebody]" with "help [somebody]." "Six months ago, I came here to help" and "I helped to cook in that factory before coming here" are expression that workers commonly use to describe their employment status and history. The following excerpt shows the use of the word *help* on the occasion of a job change, although higher pay and convenient location were the real motives for changing jobs:

> Ms. Tsai said that she left Ta-you two years ago to work in a garment factory because it paid her more. However, the garment factory is not

as close as Ta-you to where she lives. She decided to come back to Ta-you last year. "When the peak season began, I came back to help [*bangmang*]," she said.

The word *help* is most often used by the workers to show that they have made compromises in order to carry out unusual tasks. When I asked A-shiea, one of the outsiders, about the schedule for the following days, she said,

> Tonight we did not plan to work. We were planning to take tomorrow night off also. Now, since Cheng's work has to meet a deadline, we cannot refuse to help him rush it through.

From the worker's viewpoint, even though she/he has contracted to sell her/his labor upon employment, the situation in the factory usually demands extra effort. The agreement to work overtime or to change one's schedule to meet production deadlines is presented as "help," rather than as part of the employment contract. When a sixty-year-old female worker fulfilled the expectation/obligation of working overtime, she thought about her employment status, but she also believed that a personal commitment was involved.

> Ms. Chang told me that she didn't sleep well after having had too much tea while she was working overtime in the factory late last night. I told her that she should take a nap at noon. She said, "It's too short. I will have to come back to work right after lunch. I have to wait until tonight."
>
> "But you have to work overtime tonight. Can you tell Cheng [the owner] that you won't work overtime tonight?" I asked.
>
> "No. We take others' money [meaning we work for others]. Besides, he has a rush deadline. I have to help him."

The owners, however, tend to deny the reality of the workers' claim to such a personal dimension. When I asked an owner about the "help" he has been getting from the workers, he said, "I need their help and they need the money. It's that simple." In fact, the workers certainly do attach material expectations to the "help" they "offer." They often talk about their unfailing loyalty to their jobs or employer when they expect something in return from the owner. Feng-yuan, a homeworker, was really upset when the owner of her factory cut the piece rate from NT$1.4 to NT$1.3. She protested, "When he is in a crunch, I always help him out."

One female outsider explained to me how they decide their schedule in the peak season to ensure work orders in the slack season.

Her husband is the contractor. When the factories need workers, they call him up. He then decides which contracts he will accept and who goes to which factory to work. The problem she and her husband confront is that, during the peak season, there are more work orders than they can handle, whereas in the slack season there are not enough work orders, and they can hardly make a living. Therefore, factories that promise to provide them with work orders during the slack season receive preferential treatment during the busy season.

> We give their work first priority during the peak season. For example, now Mr. Li wants us to take more orders from him, but he doesn't give us any work during the slack season. . . . We can't help him. It's impossible for us to help him out by taking more orders from him now.

### The Owner's "Good Will"

The owners invest substantial amounts of their time and energy to compensate for a presumably unbalanced relationship with their workers. They do so because, although such efforts are not directly related to manufacturing production, they pay off in the long run. As owner Mr. Li put it, one of the reasons why it is so difficult to run a factory is that "many of the things we do for them [the workers] have nothing to do with our business." Yet, such extra efforts to establish personal relationships with their workers make it easier for the owners of Taiwan's satellite factories to exert control over the workers and give the owners greater leverage in the exercise of managerial power.

The owners' attempts to develop personal relationships with their workers frequently take the form of material inducements linked to the worker's private lives. For example, in Sing-sing, a box body factory, the owner's mother and wife always gave candy or cookies to the outsiders' children who accompanied their mothers to the factory. Another owner of a box body factory let a worker who lived next door take the waste wooden boards home to use as fuel to cook porridge and boil hot water. As the owner put it, "I have no use for the waste wooden boards. She works hard when I am in a crunch."

Other relationships, develop when the owners provide minor favors. For example, Chu-lin, the wife of a glass factory owner, let worker Jia-lin use their bedroom when Jia-lin needed to breast-feed her newborn baby. Owner Mr. Li went to the hospital with Bush, a mentally retarded male worker, when Bush became infected with venereal disease after visiting prostitutes. He also took A-jin's mother, a rural woman who had never been to the city, to visit the hospital where worker A-jin was hospitalized after a motorcycle accident. Li's wife agreed to buy a pack of dry bamboo shoots from her village for Show-may, a female worker who planned to cook a special dish on her father-in-law's birthday.

The owners are very aware that they stand to gain from such interventions. For example, Mr. Li had to make several trips to the local municipal court during the time worker Lie-may's husband was in prison charged with insulting a police officer while under the influence of alcohol. Lie-may's sister-in-law, A-ming, worked in the same factory, and A-ming's husband was the manager. Several times I ran across Mr. Li right after he returned from the court. He complained about how much time the case had taken up and protested that the whole thing really had nothing to do with his factory business. However, he also said, "I really have no choice. He is my worker's husband and manager's relative. What can I do? I need workers. It's impossible for me not to get involved."

## Forms of Resistance in the Satellite Factory

Countermovements on the part of workers determined to resist the owners' efforts to exploit their labor are a significant feature of labor relations in Taiwan's satellite factories. The workers seldom give up any chance to define a social environment in which they can retain a certain degree of bargaining power. They create and foster such an environment by letting it be known that they will not always comply.

### "Those Women Are Petty Minded"

The most significant tactic female workers employ to increase the possibility of getting a better deal from their employers is to engage in constant wrangling. This tactic is widely used, particularly among female outsiders and piece-rate workers. The daily exchanges these women carry on with the owner form a channel of dialogue that they believe has indirect efforts on the terms they receive.

A "wrangle" often evolves from a normal daily conversation and ends up with one party feeling the "winner" and the other the "loser." In most encounters, several female workers are involved. During a wrangle, the women apply various tactics to assist each other. These include elaborating another coworkers' point if one sees a potential weakness, joining the wrangle simply to show the coworker that she is not alone, and forming an alliance to engage in a wrangle with clear goals in mind.

Feng-yuan was one of the women who never let anybody outsmart her in a wrangle. She painted stained glass at a sweatshop at the end of an apartment building. The shop was on the corner of two alleys where women in the neighborhood usually got together in the afternoon to chat. Although the factory owner distributed and collected the glass from every homeworker's apartment in the local community, he taught only Feng-yuan how to perform the paint job when a new design was commissioned. Other women in the community had to learn how to do the painting from Feng-yuan. The owner also stored all the dyestuffs in the sweatshop. Other piece-rate homeworkers obtained daily dyestuff supplies from there.

A typical wrangle between Mr. Lai, an unmarried owner in his late thirties, and Feng-yuan, a married woman in her mid-twenties, could either get started through Mr. Lai's inquiries or through Feng-yuan's complaints. The two then bantered back and forth until one side felt that he or she had won the battle and shot the other down. During the verbal exchange, Feng-yuan was very careful about the meaning and direction of their conversation. She did not let Mr. Lai get the upper hand. For example, when Mr. Lai delivered the glass one hot summer afternoon, Feng-yuan's three-year-old daughter Chun-lien had just woken up.

> Mr. Lai told Chun-lien, who was lying down on the worktable next to Feng-yuan, "Don't sleep like that. Otherwise you won't be able to find a *pojia*.[1] Nobody is going to marry a girl who sleeps like that."
> Feng-yuan responded. "Why should you worry? You don't even have a son yet!"
> Mr. Lai remarked, "How do you know that I don't have a son?"
> Feng-yuan responded. "Oh Yeah? Unless you have a bastard."

One morning Feng-yuan told me that she had a long night because her husband had not returned home. When Mr. Lai did his morning delivery, Feng-yuan showed her moodiness.

> "I have not been in the mood to paint the glass. I fell like breaking all of them," Feng-yuan complained to Mr. Lai.
> "Breaking the glass? Go ahead! I would slap you if you dare," Mr. Lai replied.
> "Nobody dares to slap her, not even her husband," contributed Li-shiang, a woman who had been standing there listening to this ongoing verbal battle.

Mr. Lai added, "I would! She can try and see."

Following Li-shiang, Feng-yuan said, "Yeah, not even my husband dares to slap me. Unless . . . Unless you have a [intimate] relationship with me that is even closer than my husband's."

Mr. Lai was stunned and embarrassed. He became very quiet after that. I was amazed by Feng-yuan's guts.

For female workers, the wrangle is fun. They enjoy engaging in it and feel proud of their triumph, whether it results in a blush on the owner's face or a ten-cent increase on the piece rate. The women take joy and pride to recite how their boss was outwitted. The tale often reaches instantly to a wide audience. Twists and turns are occasionally spiced up as the tale travels from one circle of women to another. It is not uncommon for women talk about one specific incident for days, especially if no new ones arise. For the owner, losing a wrangle can be very embarrassing at the time, even though he might insist that there is no real winner or loser. One owner told me specifically,

> Those poor women are really petty minded. They are fooling themselves. They think they gain something by arguing with me. It is just a game. I sometimes let them feel good about themselves so that they will work hard for me.

The female workers see it differently. According to A-shiea, A-in, A-chu, and A-ju, a group of female outsiders, the hidden agenda for engaging in the wrangle is to define and defend their territory. This is very clear in their interaction with the owner of Sing-sing. Several times they privately informed me that, at the same piece rate, they would rather work at Sing-sing because the owner's wife and mother treated their children nicely whenever they brought them along. Besides, unlike some other factories, Sing-sing had a big backyard next to the rice field where their children could play with their tricycles. I asked the workers why they nevertheless always made a big fuss about the piece rate with the owner. "We do that a lot. It's just a way to make sure that they won't think we are living at their mercy," replied A-shiea.

The wrangle defines a pattern of personal interaction that can easily be transformed into a business-related negotiation. Feng-yuan jokingly protested when Mr. Lai told her to be delicate with a new design.

> "In principle, you shouldn't rush. Don't let the dye get outside of the lines. The flowers should look natural. They should be painted nicely," Mr. Lai said.

> "In principle? How dare you business guys talk about principle? Your conscience has long been eaten up by the dog. How can you talk about principles?" teased Feng-yuan.

One afternoon Mr. Lai asked Feng-yuan the whereabouts of Show-pao, another piece-rate homeworker in the neighborhood. Feng-yuan took the chance to let out her long-standing frustration. She said.

> Why should I know where she is. . . . She went out simply because she didn't like the work you just gave to her. Don't give the glass back to me. I warned you! Okay?

After talking about something else for a while, Mr. Lai again inquired about Show-pao's whereabouts.

> "Don't mention her name any more, would you! I am so sick of being the neighbor of a Hakka." Mr. Lai, a Hakka himself, said "What's wrong with being a Hakka?"
>
> "You people take advantage of others. She only does easy work and lets others do the difficult jobs. That's what's wrong," responded Feng-yuan.

Feng-yuan told me afterward that people in the neighborhood do not like Show-pai. She always takes advantage of others. Several times she asked Mr. Lai to send complicated designs to other women while she herself got the easy ones.

It is easier to win a wrangle when the women act together as a group. A-shiea, A-in, A-chu, and A-ju formed a team. As outsiders, they moved from one box body factory to another to assemble the drawers. Because they did not work for any contractor, they negotiated their own piece rate with each factory owner. Among themselves, they constantly evaluated the piece rate each factory offered against the complexity, quantity, and urgency of the contract. They usually expressed their consensus in the following terms: "Let's turn down Wu's factory. It's too far away. Besides, it has less than 2,000 pieces. It's not worth our going." The following excerpt is an example of their daily exchanges with the owner on the shop floor:

> The owner's brother came over to A-shiea, A-in, and A-chu. He told them to be careful. Otherwise, he warned. "We will withhold one dollar for every defect."
>
> A-in said, "How can you do that? You pay us only 65 cents for each drawer we make."

> A-shiea joined, "Yeah, it isn't fair. Are you saying that we are getting two dollars for every extra drawer we make?"

When they have to cut a deal with the owner, each one of them plays a delicate role in the process of negotiation.

> A-shiea complained to the owner, "The work we do for you is half paid and half free."
>
> A-in joined the conversation:
>
> "Yeah, the piece rate has been the same for many years."
>
> The owner said that the factory had given them a higher rate for the last model they made.
>
> A-shiea didn't feel the owner had responded to their complaint: "In the past, when your profit was higher, you didn't pay us better. Now the cost of living is getting higher and higher. We are still paid the same rate as before."
>
> "It is not that we didn't pay you better. We couldn't. The cost of production was higher than," said the owner.
>
> A-chu chimed in, "A-shiea is right. The work we do for you is only half paid. The other half you get for free."
>
> The owner's brother came over to tell them that they should not be so calculating. "You won't be able to take the money with you when you die anyway," he said.
>
> A-shiea replied. "That's very true. So why don't you pay us more, since you are not going to take all the money with you when you die either?"

Occasionally, the female workers spoke about the better terms they had won as the result of a wrangle. For example, one morning Feng-yuan told me that the day before she had argued with Mr. Lai until he agreed to pay her a dollar apiece. "Nobody around here believes that I can get such a good price. . . . They think I am a genius in wrangling," Feng-yuan announced with pride.

Empirically speaking, these brisk wrangles reveal an interesting, underdocumented aspect of women's lives in Taiwan. Anyone who is familiar with Taiwan's local communities can attest to the vocal temperament of Taiwanese women in rural villages, their clever bargaining skills in daily shopping, and their quarrelsome reputation in extended families. To a certain extent, therefore, it is not an overstatment for Margery Wolf to assert that men in local villages were fully aware of the danger of being tried and humiliated by these gutsy, loud, and rugged women (M. Wolf, 1972). At the conceptual level, wrangling is a daily, conscious effort that women make to resist undefined but potentially limitless claims on their labour that the owners could have imposed.

### Gossip

Although the operational rules in the satellite factory are pretty much decided upon by the owner and complied with by the workers, there is ongoing discontent among the workers. The latter are, of course, fully aware of the obvious abusive practices on the shop floor. Just the same, in most of the cases, they prudently avoid any acts of public defiance because of their vulnerable position.

According to Elson and Pearson, workers' subordination or passivity is not a natural and original state (Elson and Pearson 1981). The workers engage every day in so-called self-repression. Typically, this manifests itself as contradictory behavior. For example, workers display subservience when the supervisors are around, but ridicule them in their absence. In the satellite factories, discontent goes underground in the form of gossip. The areas of gossip include two major categories: job-related information and work-related discontent.

In Ta-you, for example, the meal allotment was a source of unrest among the workers. The workers were asked to pay meal expenses of twenty-five dollars a day: five for breakfast and ten each for lunch and dinner. They were also told that the factory would provide a matching fund of another twenty-five dollars each for workers who had their daily meals in the factory. Thus the amount of meal expenses totaled NT$50 a day per person. However, the workers were not happy with the kind of meals they were getting. One Saturday afternoon worker A-tong vented his discontent while the owner and his wife were out of town. It got started while he was eating from a lunch box in the office around two o'clock. He had bought the lunch box from a nearby store because he had returned to the factory late and there was nothing left in the kitchen.

> "Even if the company doesn't contribute the money they promised to contribute [with thirty workers], we should still have seven hundred and fifty dollars every day for our meal expenses. . . . I didn't know the owner's wife gets only six hundred dollars from Miss Shu [the bookkeeper]. . . . I think, instead of having the owner's wife do the daily shopping, it would be better if we have somebody else do it. . . . For the last few days, she didn't even bother to save something for me.

When I came back [late for lunch], there was nothing left. She simply jokingly told me that I should skip the meal as if I were on a diet. This is ridiculous. . . . Besides, look at what we have every day. Bean sprouts, cabbage, pork's head skin, and tofu. It is always four dishes without a main dish [a meat dish]. With these kinds of dishes, I doubt if she really spends all six hundred dollars," remarked A-tong.

"No, I don't think these dishes cost that much. I asked my mom once. She said they do not," added Miss Shu.

"The company not only doesn't put in the money it promises to put in; they even *eat* our money. This is too much!" exclaimed A-tong.

"If I talk to Mr. Li about this, he will ask me to get the person who makes the complaints [to talk to him]. Who do you think I should get? How can I say, 'Hey! A-tong! Come talk to Mr. Li.' You will be in real trouble [if Mr. Li Hears that it's you]," said Ms. Chang, another bookkeeper.

"You should not do a thing like that," I said, joining the conversation. "This is something that affects everyone. You should discuss this with others and present your decision to Mr. Li as a group. It's unfair to single out an individual when the issue affects everybody else. Besides, a group approach will be more effective," I added.

"A-tong, why don't you go and organize a union?" Miss Shu jokingly said.

No conclusion emerged from the conversation. However, two persons left the office with unexpected anxiety. A-tong, the outspoken worker, started to worry that somebody in the group might report him to the owner. He specifically asked me not to tell on him. I, the participant observer, felt that I might be thrown out of the field site because I had accidentally expressed a personal opinion that revealed my political stand on a certain issue.

As time went on, several signs indicated that someone in the group had reported the incident to the owner, Mr. Li. One noticeable change was in the meal arrangement for the following week. Instead of having his wife cook for the workers, Mr. Li ordered lunch boxes from a nearby take-out store for everybody. This was a major change because, in the past, only the outsiders had had the privilege of having lunch boxes; ordering a lunch box is more expensive than having the meal prepared in the factory. Although the meal arrangement returned to its previous state a week later, Mr. Li managed to let me know that he had learned about my participation in that Saturday afternoon conversation. When I left Ta-you, Mr. Li asked me if I could give him a final report regarding my observations at the factory. Specifically, he asked me to write about improvements that the factory should make. "You can talk about almost everything. Things like meal arrangements or whatever," he said.

### "He Has a Bad Temper"

When owners talk about the difficulties of running a business, they frequently mention the terrible experiences they have had with "bad-tempered" workers. In their descriptions, these workers are usually very arrogant and uncooperative. They take days off when they wish and show up at work in a bad mood. The craftsmaster Ro-pao, at Ta-you, was one of these "bad-tempered" workers.

Ro-pao had left Ta-you to start a factory with his friends two years before. When the new business was still in its early stage, Mr. Li, Ta-you's owner, invited Ro-pao to return to Ta-you. According to Ro-pao and his wife, they decided to come back in part because they were uncertain how their new business might turn out. The main attraction, however, was Mr. Li's promise of partnership with Ro-pao. Mr. Li told Ro-pao that he would become a shareholder of Ta-you. He would not only receive wages but also share the profits Ta-you makes every year.

The reason Mr. Li made such a good offer had to do with Ro-pao's craftsmanship. As a craftsmaster, Ro-pao knew how to design and make new models for potential buyers. His craft skills were valuable because, in general, it takes eight to ten years for an apprentice to master these skills and become a craftsmaster. For an assembly factory such as Ta-you, having attractive new models every year is the first step to being successful in the business. Mr. Li himself had virtually no knowledge of the craft. Therefore, it was crucial for Mr. Li to retain someone like Ro-pao. From Ro-pao's standpoint, Mr. Li's offer was very appealing because, for one thing, it promised Ro-pao treatment, wages, and profits similar to what he would have received in the new business he had just started with his friends. In addition, Ta-you had been in business for several years, and its prospects were much brighter. Ro-pao decided to take Mr. Li's offer and became Ta-you's only craftsmaster.

After Ro-pao returned, however, Mr. Li failed to carry out his promises. Ro-pao continued to work as a hired laborer and did not become one of the shareholders. Although his daily wages were much higher than the average worker's, Ro-pao still felt cheated. He acted out his bitterness by not fully applying his craft skills, instead withholding them as his private property to whatever extent possible. On the shop floor, he preferred to work as an unskilled worker. Whenever Mr. Li wanted to utilize

Ro-pao's craft skill, the tension between them escalated. Mr. Li intended to extract Ro-pao's skills, while Ro-pao tried to keep this appropriation to a minimum, if not altogether impossible. When Mr. Li's pressure reached beyond what Ro-pao felt he was willing to accept, he would show his resentment and angry feelings. He would then make any further extraction impossible by making personal interaction between himself and Mr. Li difficult. This behavior upset Mr. Li because the social distance created by Ro-pao constrained Mr. Li's control over him.

When I came across Ro-pao early one morning, he was very tense. He wore a frozen and stony look. He did not even respond to my greeting. Clearly, something had happened. I went to the office upstairs. A few minutes later, Mr. Li entered with the manager and three other key workers. During the meeting in his office, Mr Li publicly condemned the absent Ro-pao. He angrily said,

> The reason I got him back here is to have him making all the models. Now that he has a bad temper, I don't even dare to ask him to do all the things [that I want him to do]. This is ridiculous. . . . He is a craftsmaster. We need him to explore the market for us. He is not employed for [work at] the assembly line. If I want to have somebody work at the assembly line, I can get somebody [to whom] I will only pay two hundred and fifty dollars a day. . . . I can't be concerned with his temper every day. I can't treat him as a Buddha and worship and burn incense to the Buddha every day.

On other occasions, Mr. Li reiterated to me that Ro-pao had a bad temper and was quite moody most of the time. "He acts like an artist," Mr Li said.

Other owners also told me stories about the "bad-tempered" workers they have met over the years. When I first started working in Mr. Cheng's box body factory, the owner worked until one o'clock in the morning every day. His craftsmaster had just left the previous month. As a result, Mr. Cheng had to put in extra hours for the upcoming deadlines. When he talked about this craftsmaster, Cheng said,

> I gave him eight hundred dollars a day. He was still unsatisfied. He threw the boxes around when he was moody. People here think that he really has a bad temper. . . . I didn't want to argue with him. Last month, he quit. I didn't ask him to stay. Now I have to work overtime for the two orders I took on before he left.

However, the new craftsmaster Cheng hired two weeks later turned out to be "very arrogant and never admits any mistakes he makes." The craftsmaster sometimes decided to take one or two days off on his own and simply didn't show up for work. When Cheng called him at home, his mother would answer the phone and say that her son was not feeling well that day. In a glass factory a skilled worker who was described as an irresponsible person by the owner told me how the owner had come to accept his "bad temper" and to keep quiet.

> I first worked here as an apprentice. After two years, I became a craftsmaster. A year ago, I told them that I wanted to work as a piece-rate worker in the peak season and get daily wages in the slack season. They didn't like it. I remained home for three days, and then they called me. Now I can make around thirty thousand dollars a month in the peak season. In the slack season, they pay me half of that. I know they don't like it. But they are afraid of losing me. . . . I don't really care. Sometimes I go and get some drinks with my friends. If I don't come to work for several days, they [the owner and his brothers] come and look for me. As long as I return to work, they won't dare to scold me.

These descriptions of the "bad-tempered" workers suggest that to consciously make oneself unavailable for social interaction and work is a common strategy used by skilled workers to resist an owner's control. Clashes over the ownership of a worker's labor and skill are part of the daily routine on the shop floor. Temporarily terminating the normal and ongoing social interaction is a disguised form of public dissent employed by workers to resist the owner's control over their labor.

The workers involved in the clashes are almost always skilled workers. With the hierarchical division of labor between males and females, it is not a coincidence that all the "bad-tempered" workers are men. Moreover, when the owners talked about the clashes, they omitted any mention of the real reason behind the conflicts. The owner always attributed opposition to individual personality—the worker's "bad temper." Finally, the clashes are limited to the individual level. No collective bargaining takes place in the satellite factory.

## Conclusions

As I pointed out in Chapter 2, it is the people, not the regulations that define the operational mechanisms in the satellite factory. Both owners and workers expend considerable effort to add a personal dimension to an otherwise material relationship. This societal context provides the basis from which to understand the awareness, compliance, and resistance of workers in Taiwan's satellite factories.

Given the fact that, in Taiwan, unionization is illegal in factories with less than thirty workers, the struggle waged by the workers in this sector is necessarily circumspect. Anyone who regards the relatively calm surface of labor relations as evidence of harmony between workers and owners misses an important dimension of labor politics in Taiwan. With neither institutional means of resistance nor political protection, the workers in Taiwan's satellite factory system resort to informal, individualized, and clandestine methods. None of the tactics they use can successfully challenge or alter the basic structure of the system. Nor have the workers demonstrated any such intention. Worker resistance takes the form of individual efforts to carve out their own niches within an oppressive labor regime.

Moreover, the opportunities for resistance are greater for men than for women, partly because women are less likely than men to hold skilled jobs, and partly because married women, especially those with children, are bound by more intricate webs of "gratitude" to the owners of the factories.

# Conclusion

In contrast to South Korea and Singapore, which built their recent economic prosperity on large factories in export processing zones, Taiwan based its "economic miracle" on small-scale, family-centered, export-oriented satellite factories in local neighborhoods. The KMT's development policy, represented by Living Rooms as Factories, promoted a system of manufacturing that draws upon married women's productive and reproductive labor. Although many of the first cohort of Taiwanese factory daughters left large factories upon marriage, their careers as factory workers were not terminated, as suggested by the concept "part-time proletarian" proposed by Gates (1987). Under the satellite factory system women are simultaneously converted into wives, mothers, and daughters-in-law on the one hand, and waged, unwaged, and casual homeworkers on the other. Unlike the rural women who depended on the "uterine family" for their well-being when Margery Wolf conducted her research in the 1960s, the married women of the 1970s and 1980s were pressed to live up to an image propagated by the state; that is, they were expected to be pretty women, lovely wives, responsible mothers, and diligent workers. The intertwining of the family and the factory characterizes the latest version of the Chinese family. Through it, married women's labor is appropriated for the international market.

Even though manufacturing in both Italy and Taiwan has recently made major advances, an "economic miracle" that is commanded by the principle of Living Room as Factories represents a non-craft-based production that, in many respects, is distinctively different from the Italian craft-based production described by Piore and Sabel (1984). Taiwan's satellite factory system gets its competitive edge from oppressive labor practices and severe labor control, whereas the competitiveness of craft-based production of the Italian variety derives from technological innovation. Although neither the craft-based nor the non–craft-based system of production is unionized, the operational mechanism of the former is decentralized, while the latter is centralized and paternalistic.

Because Taiwan's export-led economy rests on small-scale manufacturers, Taiwanese workers have had a chance to escape their proletarian status by opening their own factories. Statistics show that men, rather than women, have benefited from such opportunities. A working-class married woman may experience upward mobility only when her husband becomes an owner. Such mobility, nevertheless, seldom leads to gender equality. The productive labor of women who marry factory owners is more likely to be unrewarded, in monetary terms, than is the labor of the wives of employed workers in the private sector. The existence of what Gates calls an "inflated petty bourgeoisie" therefore implies that class equality has been achieved by persistent gender inequality. Women whose husbands are wage workers need paid employment because of their husbands' low wages. The ways they are integrated into the satellite factory system vary according to their childbearing and child-rearing responsibilities. At different stages in life, they are wage workers, casual workers, or homeworkers.

Several recent studies that look at the petty capitalist mode of production in Taiwan underline two further themes pertinent to my analysis. The first concerns the societal basis of the capitalist-worker relationship. In *Market, Social Networks, and the Production Organization of Small-Scale Industry in Taiwan,* Chih-Ming Ka (1993) focuses on the manufacture of garments for Taiwan's working-class and lower-middle-class consumers. Ka finds that this sector is labor intensive but requires constant adaptation to seasonal fashion. Thus a relatively small profit margin is maximized through tight labor control. To stay competitive, Ka finds, factory owners must call upon a social mechanism that ensures personal loyalty to reduce labor turnover and increase productivity. The owners make frequent trips to their home villages to recruit daughters of acquaintances and extended family members. These young girls, according to one owner's description are "diligent, docile, willing to take orders, and to work overtime. They often stay [work for you] till they are married" (Ka 1993, 87). Furthermore, personal ties with the owners make these young women hesitate to find out how they might otherwise have been paid and treated in the current job market. In Taiwan's export shoe industry, Ian Skoggard documents similar mechanisms through which the true nature of capitalist relations and practices is concealed behind traditional social relations (Skoggard 1993).

The second major theme underlying recent studies of Taiwan's petty capitalist production is the incorporation of gender analysis. For example, Skoggard documents a clear gender division of labor in Taiwan's export shoe industry. He shows that gender inequality is manifested there in its most familiar forms. That is, female workers still earn a lot less than male workers. Women are assigned to more labor-intensive tasks and have fewer chances to be promoted (Skoggard 1993). In Taiwan's domestic garment production, a sector that relies primarily on women's labor and skills, Ka (1993) and Y.-T. Li and Ka (1994) find that many male owners enter the business simply because their wives have access to invaluable resources. After working in the sector for years prior to their marriage, the wives not only have acquired technological know-how, but quite often have also established personal ties to networks of marketing and production. These resources lay a solid foundation for an enterprise's future success. No wonder some male owners attribute their head start to the "dowry" their wives brought into their marriage, whereas others jokingly refer to themselves as people who benefit from their wives' apron-string relationship. Apart from the vital social resources they bring into their marriages, the owners' wives contribute productive labor that is indispensable to the daily operation of a family business. Most important, the wives are the soul of research and development, which relies on their expertise in making clothes to explore or take on new lines of seasonal fashion.

My examination of labor politics and gender stratification in Taiwan's satellite factory system introduces some new perspectives. First of all, it clearly shows that the employer-worker relationship cannot be perceived as simply a renewed application of traditional practices. Instead, one needs to look at the political context that helps to shape the relationship between bosses and workers. In Taiwan's case, the KMT's pro-capitalist labor policies have made it possible for the capitalists to take the law into their own hands. Furthermore, although I agree with Ka and Skoggard that factory owners enjoy the upper hand in their manipulation of the worker-employer relationship, it is misleading to assume that the owners are the sole players, and therefore always in full control. By using ethnographic data to examine various facets of the relationship, I have been able to demonstrate that the workers are neither naive nor passive about the exploitative aspect of their relationship with the owners. In fact, on the shop floor, workers consciously engage in vigorous negotiation and calculated resistance, notwithstanding their relatively powerless position vis-à-vis their employer. Moreover, as a result of job stratification, one can differentiate tactics employed by male and female workers in their daily struggles. My findings echo James C. Scott's work on tactics used by the less powerful to defy control of the more powerful (Scott 1990). My analysis of labor relations in Taiwan's satellite factories has convinced me that the notion of worker resistance, conventionally defined in terms of collective and large-scale movements, must be broadened.

I conclude that an analysis of gender stratification must do more than examine the productive or reproductive labor of married women. Rather, we must explore the linkage and tensions between productive and reproductive labor and look closely at the process through which married women are made to take on multiple duties. In Taiwan, both productive and reproductive labor are appropriated for economic development under the name of Living Rooms as Factories and through the doctrine of Mothers' Workshops. The complicated schedules adopted by married women attest to their effort to accommodate their productive and reproductive responsibilities. Women's recollections of their trying moments during the first years of marriage reveal the excruciating process through which married women are converted into waged or unwaged workers.

In addition to portraying married women's emotions and struggles, I have tried to disentangle the interplay of women's gender and class identities. In my analysis, I identify two groups of women: those who experience upward mobility by marrying into the owners' families and those who remain homeworkers and wage workers. While women in both groups acknowledge gender inequality despite their divergent class affiliation, this acknowledgement is not sufficient to forge an alliance between them when their class interests are at stake. Ethnographic data further indicate that the owners' wives experience persistent tension between their gender and class identities. I have become convinced that, to conceptualize class and gender struggles among groups as well as within groups, we must focus on women's own understandings of their roles as both workers and wives.

My original analysis of the satellite factory system, based on the data I collected during my 1989–90 field trips, was substantially completed in the summer of 1991. Between then and the summer of 1992 when I returned to Taiwan, the implications for Taiwan's export industry of a growing labor shortage and rising labor costs were hotly debated. The general consensus was that Taiwan's economic development had reached a bottleneck, since labor was no longer cheap and plentiful. Among the proposed solutions, the KMT government emphasized long-term solutions: industrial advancement through automation and technological upgrading. The manufacturers, however, focused on short-term alleviation. Requests to import foreign workers ran parallel with calls for the abolition of the government's ban on capital relocation to China. In the meantime, Taiwan's capitalist producers were secretly shifting their investment from Taiwan to Southeast Asia and China, and reports on illegal workers from Malaysia, Thailand, and China made newspaper headlines. In 1990 the KMT government finally gave 1,500 lines of labor-intensive production the green light to relocate to China. By the end of the year a total of US$1.7 to 1.8 billion in investment had shifted to China (CIER 1991, 262). One year later, the importation of foreign workers was legalized. These changes indicate that Taiwan is evolving into a new economic era. Exactly how this will affect the satellite factory system and people in that system is still uncertain.

My 1992 trip to Taiwan and China enabled me to revisit the satellite factories in which I had worked before, and also to look in on a number of factories recently established by Taiwanese entrepreneurs in China. Before my arrival, I was unsure whether the factories I had worked in three years earlier would still be in business. It turned out that of the six factories, four were still in the same line of production. One had closed down without leaving a trace, and another had shifted to a new line of business. According to a factory owner, the system had reached a bottleneck, and his line of work represented a "sunset industry." "Its ultimate decline is only a matter of time," he said. Most owners expressed similar somber sentiments when they talked about the future prospects of their factories. Profits in the wooden jewelry box industry dropped from 40–50 percent in the early 1980s to 10–15 percent in the early 1990s. Technological innovation or upgrading was out of the question because investment in factory automation simply does not pay off. Some owners who had been in manufacturing for years gradually lost their drive and diverted their profits to real estate or the stock market. With wages accounting for up to 50 percent of production costs, others entertained the possibility of hiring foreign workers or relocating their production to areas with cheap and plentiful labor.

The hardware factory was making one shipment every other week to China, because some of its clients had moved there. The young manager and his brother had taken over the family business from their father the previous year. The family business was still running, but the co-owner was not very optimistic about the future.

> By moving Taiwanese factories to China, we may be able to keep the business going for a while. . . . I don't know what will happen once they [people in China] learn the skills and take over the business. . . . People like us would be caught in the middle. Honestly speaking, I don't think anybody would offer me a job. I am not a technician. Neither do I have the credentials to be hired by the big corporations.

A few weeks prior to my return visit he had decided to take computer-programming classes at night "to see if I can catch the last train toward technology upgrade."

Because of time constraints, I did not attempt to locate every woman I met on my previous trips. From the few with whom I did have a chance to reconnect, I learned that married women's work and family lives continue to be shaped by the outcomes of their negotiations with the capitalist system and with patriarchal norms.

Ms. Chang, who had treated me to the bitter melon, was still doing much the same kind of work. In the two-year period, she had "helped" at a leather factory for a year or so, before taking up her current job in a wooden furniture factory assisting a craftsman in cutting and carving wooden boards. "The work in the leather factory was more exhausting and dangerous," she said. According to her, the matchmaker was still active in matchmaking but had retired from factory work to look after her grandchildren at home.

Jinling, worker 22 in Table 3.6, still lived next door to the previous site of Ta-you, which now housed a residential unit. She quit her job in July 1991 when her mother had a heart attack and was hospitalized.[1] For about six months, Jinling went back and forth daily between hospital and home (a motorcycle ride of 45 minutes each way). Her mother came back home in early January 1992 and died four months later. Because she could no longer rely on her mother to cook and look after the children, Jinling got a job doing homework for a raincoat factory through her cousin whose husband worked in the factory.

Another homeworker, Lang-Lang, now worked at two jobs. According to her sister-in-law Lu, in early 1990 Lang-Lang's husband came down with an illness that the local doctors couldn't diagnose. As his health deteriorated, Lang-Lang stopped the homework and took care of her husband around the clock. Lang-Lang was gradually worn out by her husband's illness. Without homework, she was also short of money. Frustrated, exhausted, and feeling insecure, Lang-Lang asked her father-in-law to give them their share of the family property. The request was turned down by the father-in-law and the oldest brother. Lang-Lang then left her husband and children and got a job in a footwear factory at the Tanzi Export Processing Zone. Side by side with mostly young single women, Lang-Lang worked shifts and lived in the factory dormitory. She visited home once a week. Ever since, the father-in-law has turned his back on her. After her husband's death six months later, Lang-Lang moved back to her own family. She did piecework at a factory across the street in the morning and continued working the night shift at the footwear factory in the Tanzi Export Processing Zone. Her father-in-law did put aside one million dollars in the bank, but under the name of her two small children. Every month, he gives Lang-Lang the interest, but he has been heard to say that "she would never be allowed to touch the money."

As Lu recalled what was happening in her family and to Lang-Lang, she commented:

> Women are really worthless. If they say you are a bad woman, you are finished. I have learned to keep my mouth shut. Now I don't do work at home [meaning at the factory run by her husband, husband's older brother, and father-in-law]. I come here and work. It's much simpler. I don't bother to know what's going on there [the family-run factory].

While many women continued to be preoccupied by factory work and family responsibilities, others' lives took new forms. Even during my brief stay, I could not but note the massive flourishing of the sex industry. Massage parlors and barbershops that provided sex to their male clients put out extravagant street signs. I was told that "special services" to male customers were now expected from waitresses in bars, tea shops, and even some restaurants. Although most of these jobs were filled by young single women, married women I met in the satellite factory were also affected. The tailor who used to work in her brother's glass factory opened her own tailoring shop in 1990. According to her, the main business has come from several big massage parlors and barbershops in the nearby city that dressed their young female employees in fashionable sexy uniforms.

> I never go to these places to take measurements of these girls, for I have converted to Buddhism. My sister had gone there for me. She said that most of these places are in the basement of large buildings. It's really dim there even during the day. I once made a hundred backless high-slit long gowns for one shop. I really don't see how people can have that kind of life.

Feng-yuan, the young homeworker who was very gutsy in wrangling, had stopped painting glass two years before 1992. Ever since, she had been moving from one massage parlor and barbershop to another as a cook. Feng-yuan went to the market every day around seven in the morning, but she did not go to cook until ten o'clock and usually could make it back home around one in the afternoon. For the dinner shift, she went there around five. After doing the dishes, she prepared snacks for the women who served the male clients on the night shift. She usually got home around ten. According to Feng-yuan, her wages were about average. The best thing about her job was that her employers gave her a fixed amount of money for daily grocery shopping. After a while, she learned to get enough groceries both for the shop and for her own family within the fixed amount. She could therefore save her wages for other household expenses. The only drawback was that

> after a while, they [the male bosses or managers] want more from me. Men are the same. They seem to never get it enough. I usually play innocent. Before things get out of hand, I quit. . . . I know this won't last very long. Maybe I should become a hairdresser or a tailor someday.

The woman who had been given only two permissions to visit her natal family discovered that her husband kept a masseuse as mistress. The manager's wife of an assembly factory protested out loud during my return visit, "Ms. Hsiung, we got to talk. He [the husband] has abandoned his old lady. He is chasing after the twenty-something." The husband smiled but denied the charge. "She simply makes it up. How can I afford it?" he said. His eighteen-year-old niece, the daughter of workers 8 and 9 in Table 3.6, was said to be "dressed up and earning easy money."

Across the Taiwan Strait, China's economic reforms have been boosted by Taiwanese and Hong Kong capital. Special economic zones in the coastal cities are filled with young girls recruited from rural areas. In June 1992, I accompanied my parents on a visit to their home villages, Sangcheng and Taikang, in Henan, a province in midwestern China. In Sangcheng, where no running water and limited electricity were available, I was surprised to see a note calling for factory workers posted on a dirt wall outside a peasant's house: "Good News! Contact me if you know how to operate an electric sewing machine and want to do factory work in Shenzheng [one of the most rapidly growing cities in Guangdong province]. Two hundred dollars monthly wages. No restriction on age." Before we left, one of my female cousins, who had been selling firewood collected from the hillside for two or three dollars (40 to 60 U.S. cents) a day, told me that her parents wanted her to go to the factory. I told her not to go because young girls are exploited in the factory, and some are sold into prostitution. I spent long hours talking to my uncle and aunt. The morning we were leaving, my uncle, retired from the Red Army, held my hands and promised, "My dear niece. We trust you. We won't send her to the factory then." My aunt, with knitted brows, said, "But . . . but what can we do? We have a whole family here . . ."

Several months later, I received a letter from my cousin, who had indeed begun to work in a garment factory in Shanghai.

> The factory has about 300 workers. . . . There were 26 of us who left the village together. We now live in the dormitory; sixteen of us share one room. The youngest girls are 13 years old. . . . Whenever they think of their moms, they cry. . . . I didn't want to leave my parents either. But such experience could be good for me. It is a chance to learn something on my own. . . . The sky is blue. I want to work hard. Maybe someday I will be able to fly.

In subsequent letters, she told me that she left the garment factory after four months: "Room and board were all they provided. They said I was slow in learning." Joining thousands of others, she made a trip to Shenzheng, Guangdong, to try her luck there. As it turned out, she only barely made it back home, after weeks of searching unsuccessfully for a "regular job." Luck and wit alone had enabled her to escape several traps and harassments that would have forced her into prostitution.

On my way to the special economic zone, the bus took me through different parts of Xieman in Fujian province. Newly constructed apartment buildings lined the highway, while farm houses were scattered through the rice fields and garden patches along our route. One of my fellow passengers, a woman dressed in typical rural clothes, asked the person next to her for directions. As she showed her neighbor the note with the address of the place she was looking for, I overhead her comment: "My uncle is a manager at——factory. He got me a job there." In this, as in many other ways, my visit to Xieman, China, reminded me very much of the early stages of Taiwan's economic development, when large factories that employed young single women from the countryside were the norm.

The economic boom experienced by China in the last few years has captured the eyes of the world and has raised enormous expectations. Nevertheless, based on what I learned in the course of my research on class and gender relations in Taiwan's satellite factory system, I would urge a certain caution when assessing recent developments in China. As far as the Taiwanese factories that have been established there are concerned, I would want to question the methods used by Taiwanese bosses to convert a socialist labor force to capitalist production, to examine how preexisting communist sociopolitical structures are used when Taiwanese factories are set up in local communities, and to explore how these new enterprises alter, transform, or perpetuate class and gender relations. My study of the satellite factory system in Taiwan cannot, of course, provide a complete explanation of what is currently happening in China, nor does it enable us to foretell the course that Chinese economic development will take in the future. What it does is to give us a better idea about what questions to ask.

As the Taiwanese struggle to transform their economy from one based on labor-intensive manufacturing for export to one dominated by high technology and trading, the relationship between women, the state, and economic development embodied in the Living Rooms as Factories program will be called into question. Indeed, the satellite factory system may be nearing its end. There is little doubt, however, that capitalist exploitation and patriarchal subordination will continue to form the main axes of tension, conflict, and struggle in Taiwan's manufacturing sector. It remains to be seen how Taiwanese women as a group will be affected by the government's recent decision to import foreign workers and permit the relocation of capital, how single and married women of different age groups will cope with these changes, and how the transformation of the economy will alter the lives of the men and women who once worked in the satellite factory system. Meanwhile, the stories of individual women told in this book will continue to unfold.

# Notes

## Introduction

1. The First, Second, and Third worlds were terms that came out of the cold war period, when the United States and the Soviet Union were the leaders of the first/capitalist and second/communist worlds, respectively. Although the boundary between the two had begun to crumble in 1989–90 when I undertook the fieldwork for this study, and the cold war era has since been replaced by a phase often referred to as globalization, I have continued to use this terminology in order to capture the economic relationships of that historical period. Developing countries of the Third World are countries other than the United States, Canada, Japan, Australia, New Zealand, South Africa, the nations of Western Europe, and the communist areas in Europe and Asia. Assignment of countries follows that of the European Economic Community (*Statistical Abstract of the United States,* 1980, p. 876).

2. Generally speaking, large international and indigenous corporations dominate Singapore and Korea, while small factories characterize the experiences of Taiwan and Hong Kong. For a detailed discussion of these differences, see Castells (1992).

3. Diamond's fieldwork was done in 1970 (Diamond 1979, 319), Arrigo's articles use data collected in 1975 and 1977 (Arrigo 1984, 100). Kung did her fieldwork from January 1974 to January 1975 (Kung 1984, 96).

4. In my article "Between Bosses and Workers: The Dilemma of a Keen Observer and a Vocal Feminist," I compare and contrast my fieldwork experiences with that of the First World feminist researchers who entered Asian societies as "foreigners" and draw attention to certain less comprehensive and nonsystematic fieldwork accounts in the field of Asian studies (Hsiung, forthcoming).

5. For a discussion of the intersections between capitalism and patriarchy, see Heidi Hartmann (1979).

6. Although I agree with Diamond that rural women's roles in the productive sphere deserve more attention than they have received in Margery Wolf's work, women's reproductive labor is relatively more important in agricultural than in industrial economies (Diamond, 1975).

7. In the 1960s and 1970s, through the Women's Department and the Chinese Women's Antiaggression League—a semiofficial organization—middle-class women were encouraged to take part in voluntary activities such as sewing clothing for military personnel and collecting or donating cash, clothes, and foodstuffs for needy military dependents. At the same time, they were discouraged from participating in paid employment (Diamond 1973a, 1973b, 1975).

8. Niehoff (1987) has argued that individual peasant households established small factories as a way of defying state control, but it is not clear from my fieldwork observation that this was an intentional/conscious/political decision, rather than an economic choice. Moreover, only in recent years have developments in the political arena shown that independent entrepreneurs are beginning to challenge the KMT's dominant political position.

9. The diligence of Chinese people has been recorded by Western missionaries and observers since the 19th century. Steven Harrell provides a thorough survey of these early observations (Harrell 1985).

10. Class theorists traditionally argue that the class status of married women should be derived from their husbands or fathers, since women have an intermittent and limited commitment to the labor market. They also maintain that the family, rather than the individual, should be the basic unit of the class system and that the husband's class status should define the family status as well as the wife's position in the system (Goldthorpe 1983). Feminist scholars denounce such propositions as "intellectual sexism," for they make women invisible and irrelevant (Acker 1973)

## Chapter 1

1. For a detailed discussion of various structural disadvantages experienced by the aborigines in Taiwan, see Hsiung (1990).

2. Teenage prostitution has concerned many women's groups in Taiwan. Under pressure from these groups, a police station in Taipei arrested about 900 teenage prostitutes during the first six months of 1989. About 20 percent of the arrested were aboriginal, although the aborigines constitute less than 2 percent of Taiwan's population (Hsiung 1990).

3. For a more thorough analysis of class and ethnic relations in Taiwan, see Hill Gates (1981). Gates focuses mainly on the period before the mid-1980s when the opposition Democratic Progressive Party, a leading Hakka and Taiwanese party, first began effectively to challenge KMT rule. The political landscape, notably the relationship between mainlanders and Taiwanese, continues to change dramatically. The dominant position of the KMT, which represents the mainlanders, is crumbling as a result of internal conflicts and external attacks from the opposition party (Shijie Ribao, September 10, 1993).

4. Because of protests from the aborigines, since the early 1980s the term has been replaced by Yuan zu min, meaning "the natives."

5. Although there are large, capital-intensive heavy industries in the export sector (shipbuilding, petrochemicals, basic metal, machine tools, etc.), these are monopolized by the state (Scitovsky 1986, 145). Detailed discussion of the dominant role of the public sector in Taiwan's manufacturing industry can be found in Amsden (1979) and Haggard and Cheng (1987).

6. In the early 1970s the KMT strategically promoted rural-based industries in order to decrease the level of rural-urban migration and to lower production costs by fully utilizing the raw materials and the labor force in the countryside. Under the Accelerated Rural Development Program started in 1973, one of the proposed goals was "encouraging the establishment of new industries in rural areas." Employment opportunities in rural areas increased as a result. For 1966–1971 and 1972–1976, rural employment in manufacturing rose 13.5 percent and 12.2 percent, while employment in urban manufacturing rose 16.9 percent and 8 percent in the same periods (Myers 1986).

7. Factories with less than five employees are excluded from this comparison because they are not registered in the Korean census.

8. K.-L. Huang's (1984) study shows that the situation in family businesses is worse than in large corporations either Taiwanese or foreign-owned. Government-run enterprises are only slightly better.

9. The abrupt drop for male age group 20 to 24 may be due to the two to three years compulsory military service for men, beginning at age 20.

## Chapter 2

1. A critical study of the Community Development Program can be found in "Women, Export-Oriented Growth, and the State: The Case of Taiwan" by Cheng and Hsiung (1992). We show that women are excluded from the program at the organizational level, as well as being barred from political participation in their local communities.

2. This article was first published in 1973. It has been reprinted in many government publications about the Community Development Program.

3. These include two textbooks, *Supplementary Readings for the Mothers' Workshops* and *Mothers Readers II,* and one film, "Activities of the Mothers' Workshops" (Sili 1985).

4. The survey gathered information from three groups of individuals: 108 administrators, 1,265 individuals who had been directly involved in decision making at the local community level, and 1,526 local residents who were not directly involved in the Community Development Programs.

5. Because the Mothers' Workshops program is part of the Community Development Program, a community may have implemented the latter while ignoring the former. A high community sponsor rate indicates the wide distribution of the Mothers' Workshops.

6. This orientation has brought severe criticism from the state officials. As one state official put it, "Some local communities conducted their workshops with a focus on such trivial activities and forgot about the main objectives of the program" (Zhao 1984, 24–27).

7. I agree with arguments made recently that decreases in family size were not solely due to the family planning program initiated by the state in Taiwan and China (Gates 1993). However, contraceptive devices provided by the state and family planning campaigns were among the important factors that contributed to the ultimate decline.

8. Unfortunately, this survey did not ask equivalent questions about the Mothers' Workshops.

9. In addition to funding from the central government and the local office, the local community also receives donations from private organizations (Taiwan Shengzhengfu Yanjiu Kaohe FazhanWeiyuanhui 1983, 75–76). Unfortunately, data on the proportion of these private donations are not available.

10. The standard wage was NT$294 per day or NT$8,820 per month (Taiwan Shengzhengfu Gongbao, 1990).

11. The average annual expenditure of individuals in the bottom 10 percent of the income distribution was used as the basic living standard.

12. Some of the disputes have involved employers paying their workers in goods or manufactured products instead of currency.

13. A government record for 1986 shows that, among factories with more than thirty workers, only 22 percent are unionized.

## Chapter 3

1. Unfortunately, a breakdown of involuntary job losses by gender is not available in published form at this point.

2. Fruit of the areca plant. It is prepared with lime paste (calcium oxide) and, in Southeast Asia, wrapped in a peppery leaf. Enjoyed as "Chinese chewing gum," it is very popular among working-class Chinese. It has been proven, however, that betel nut has undesirable long-term health effects such as cancer of the mouth (Myer 1990).

3. The exchange rate at the time of my fieldwork in 1989 was US$1 = between NT$25 and 26.

4. In revolutionary China, the Communist Party used land reform to gain the support of male peasants by allowing them to become patriarchs within their households (Johnson 1983; Stacey 1983).

## Chapter 4

1. The possibility of not being worshipped at any shrine when one dies is a serious matter in Chinese society. Margery Wolf discusses customs that take care of the soul of single women (M. Wolf 1972, 148). A study of nuns in Taiwan shows that nuns, as well as prostitutes, form alliances modeled on those of adoptive mothers and daughters for mutual support, and particularly for ensuring that their souls will be cared for after death (Tsung 1978, 344–53). The concern also came up in a conversation with a close friend of mine who has been divorced for some time and has no prospect of getting married again. She said that her mother has discussed with her older brother the possibility of having his children worship the aunt's soul when she dies. My friend said, "My mother was really relieved when my brother agreed."

2. According to Ding, suitable marriage ages for women with different educational backgrounds are as follows: 27 for college graduates, 25 for junior high graduates, and 23 for junior and elementary school graduates (Ding 1984, 14).

3. Divorced women are considered moral failures. Young unmarried women resent them when they reenter the marital pool to compete for potential husbands,

while currently married women are afraid that the divorcees may "steal" their husbands (Arrigo 1984, 143; Shi 1987, 11).

4. Of course, within the same system, both males and females suffer from a poor education. Females, however, pay a higher price because of the double standard widespread in Chinese society and the society's rigid control over women's sexuality. As a female teacher, who gained "a questionable reputation" after having numerous boyfriends without settling down, once put it, "Being a woman is a sad business. . . . What a burden it is to be a Chinese woman born in this century, when you can't do what a man can do, when you're supposed to be either an old maid with no love interests or a woman married to a bore" (Lin 1988, 134–35).

5. A factory owner believes that the government's family-planning program has impaired the future prospects of Taiwan's satellite factory system because not as many sons will be available to inherit the family business.

6. Marrying someone of the same surname is considered incest according to Chinese custom (Lang 1946, 33).

### Chapter 5

1. Foreign buyers generally pay 20 percent to 30 percent of the total amount when they place an order. The remainder is paid when final products are delivered. In recent years, because of the depreciation of the U.S. dollar and the high level of fluctuation in foreign exchange rates, American buyers, who make up the majority of the foreign purchasers, often found themselves paying a lot more when the final products were delivered. Hence they preferred to shorten the delivery period, from three months to one month.

2. In the slack season, workers work eight hours a day, five and a half days a week.

3. Continuing working after nine o'clock in the evening is more common in assembly factories than in wooden body factories. In the wooden body factories where boards are cut and carved, working late can be extremely hazardous. Mrs. Lu, wife of the owner of a wooden body factory, lost two fingers in 1988. Mr. Lo, a craftsman, lost four fingers in 1987. Except under special circumstances, workers in the wooden body factory usually work until nine o'clock in the evening.

4. An unconfirmed source told me that the majority of factories employ the monthly type of calculation.

5. Some married couples send their children away to stay with in-laws or relatives in their hometown. This practice is especially common during the peak season.

6. I prefer the term *patriarchy* in this text because *paternalism* is generally used mainly when dealing with issues of labor control.

### Chapter 6

1. Literally, *pojia* means "mother-in-law's household." When the Chinese inquire whether a young woman is married, they ask if her parents have found her a *pojia*.

### Conclusion

1. Jinling was responsible for taking care of her mother. Because there was no son in the family, her mother chose Jinling to carry on the family name by taking in a husband. Her two sisters were married out, with dowries. By taking a husband in, Jinling was treated like a son who would inherit the family property after her mother's death. Instead of taking the husband's family name, her son took Jinling's family name.

# References

Acker, Joan. 1973. Women and social stratification: A case of intellectual sexism. *American Journal of Sociology* 78:174–83.

Acker, Joan, et al. 1991. Objectivity and truth: Problems in doing feminist research. In *Beyond methodology: Feminist scholarship as lived research*, ed. M. M. Fonow and J. A. Cook. Bloomington and Indianapolis: Indiana University Press.

Aird, John S. 1990. *Slaughter of the innocents: Coercive birth control in China*. Washington, DC: AEI Press.

Amsden, Alice H. 1979. Taiwan's economic history: A case of étatisme and a challenge to dependency theory. *Modern China* 5(3):341–80.

Arrigo, Linda Gail. 1980. The industrial workforce of young women in Taiwan. *Bulletin of Concerned Asian Scholars* 12:25–34.

———. 1984. Taiwan electronics workers. In *Lives: Chinese working women*, ed. Mary Sheridan and Janet W. Salaff, 135–45. Bloomington: Indiana University Press.

Barret, Richard E., and Martin K. Whyte. 1982. Dependency theory and Taiwan: Analysis of a deviant case. *American Journal of Sociology* 87(5):1064–89.

Benería, Lourdes, and Martha Roldan. 1987. *The crossroads of class and gender: Industrial homework, subcontracting, and household dynamics in Mexico City*. Chicago: University of Chicago Press.

Bennholdt-Thomsen, Veronika. 1988. Why do housewives continue to be created in the Third World too? In *Women: The last colony*, ed. Maria Mies, Veronika Bennholdt-Thomsen, and Claudia von Werlhof, 159–67. London: Zed Books.

Bookman, Ann. 1988. Unionization in an electronics factory: The interplay of gender, ethnicity, and class. In *Women and the politics of empowerment*, ed. Ann Bookman and Sandra Morgen, 159–79. Philadelphia: Temple University Press.

Burawoy, Michael. 1985. *The politics of production: Factory regimes under capitalism and socialism*. London: Verso.

Bureau of Statistics, Directorate-General of Budget, Accounting, and Statistics (DG-BAS), Executive Yuan. 1987. *Statistical yearbook of the Republic of China, 1987*. Taipei: Bureau of Statistics, DGBAS, Executive Yuan.

Castells, Manuel. 1992. Four Asian tigers with a dragon head: A comparative analysis of the state, economy, and society in Asian Pacific rim. In *States and development in the Asian Pacific rim,* ed. Richard P. Appelbaum and Jeffrey Henderson, 33–70. Newbury Park, CA: Sage.

Census Office of the Executive Yuan, Republic of China. 1972. *An extract report on the 1970 sample census of population and housing, Taiwan-Fukien area, R.O.C.* Taipei: Census Office of the Executive Yuan.

————. 1977. *An extract report on the 1975 sample census of population and housing, Taiwan-Fukien area, R.O.C.* Taipei: Census Office of the Executive Yuan.

————. 1982. *An extract report on the 1980 sample census of population and housing, Taiwan-Fukien area, R.O.C.* Taipei: Census Office of the Executive Yuan.

Cemada, George P., et al. 1986. Implications for adolescent sex education in Taiwan. *Studies in Family Planning* 17(4):181–87.

Chang, Sheng-ling. 1990. Nukong yu yundong: Cong zhuzhi dongyuan yu yishi rentong fenxi zhiyi nugong gonghui gean (Female workers and the labor movement: A case study of a female garment workers' union, their consciousness, their union, and the union's organization). A paper presented at Taiwan Shehui Yaundong de Huigu yu Zhanwan Yantaohui (Conference on the Past and Prospects of Taiwan's Social Movement), July 7–8, 1990, Taipei.

Chang, Y.L. 1988. Booming economy: The small entrepreuer in Taiwan. *Free China Review* 38(7):18–23.

Chen, Jie-Xuan. 1991. The economic structure of social characteristics of Taiwan's small and medium size enterprises. Ph.D. dissertation, Department of Sociology, Tunghai University.

Chen, Qi-Nan, and Shu-Ru Qiu. 1984. Qiye zhuzhi de jiben xingtai yu chuantong jianzhu zhidu (The basic structure of entrepreneur organization and family system). In *Zhongguo shi guanli* (The Chinese style of management), ed. Gongshang Shibao Jingying Chongshu Xiaozu, 457–84. Taipei: Shibao Wenhua Chuban Shiye Youxian Kongsi.

Cheng, Lucie, and Gary Gereffi. 1994. U.S. retailers and Asian garment production. In *Global production: The apparel industry in the Pacific rim,* ed. Edna Bonacich et al., 63–79. Philadelphia: Temple University Press.

Cheng, Lucie, and Ping-Chun Hsiung. 1992. Women, export-oriented growth, and the state: The case of Taiwan. In *State and development: Asian Pacific rim,* ed. Richard Appelbaum and Jay Henderson, 233–66. Beverly Hills, CA: Sage.

Chiang, Lan-hung Nora, and Yenlin Ku. 1985. *Past and current status of women in Taiwan.* Taipei: National Taiwan University, Women's Research Program.

Chou, Bier. 1989. Industrialization and change in women's status: A reevaluation of some data from Taiwan. In *Taiwan: A newly industrialized state,* ed. Hsin-huang Michael Hsiao, Wei-yuan Cheng, and Hou-sheng Chan. Taipei: Department of Sociology, National Taiwan University.

Chou, Tein-Chen. 1985. *Industrial organization in the process of economic development: The case of Taiwan, 1950–1980.* Louvain-la-Neuve, Belgium: CIACO.

Chung-hua Institution for Economic Research (CIER). 1991. *Haixia liangan jingmao hudong zhi yujing shuliang maxing ji yingyong* (Trading-warning system for monitoring Taiwan-China economic interdependence and its applications). Taipei: Chung-hua Institution for Economic Research.

Cohen, Myron L. 1976. *House united, house divided: The Chinese family in Taiwan.* New York: Columbia University Press.

Cole, Robert E. 1971. *Japanese blue collar: The changing tradition.* Berkeley: University of California Press.

Deyo, Frederic C. 1987. State and labor: Modes of political exclusion in East Asian development. In *The political economy of the new Asian industrialism,* ed. Frederic C. Deyo. Ithaca, NY: Cornell University Press.

———. 1989. *Beneath the miracle: Labor subordination in the new Asia–industrialism.* Berkeley: University of California Press.

Diamond, Norma. 1969. *Kun Shen: A Taiwan village.* New York: Holt, Rinehart and Winston.

———. 1973a. The middle class family model in Taiwan: Woman's place is in the home. *Asian Survey* 13:853–72.

———. 1973b. The status of women in Taiwan: One step forward, two steps back. In *Women and China: Studies in social change and feminism,* ed. Marilyn B. Young. Ann Arbor: University of Michigan Press.

———. 1975. Women under Kuomintang rule: Variations of the feminine mystique. *Modern China* 1(1):3–45.

———. 1979. Women and industry in Taiwan. *Modern China,* 5(3):317–40.

Ding, Sumeng. 1984. Danshen nuzi de xinli (The psychological aspects of single women). *Jengkang Shijie* (Healthy world) 103:6–18.

Directorate-General of Budget, Accounting, and Statistics (DGBAS), Executive Yuan. 1972. *The report on 1971 industrial and commercial census, Taiwan-Fukien area, the Republic of China,* vol. 3. Taipei: Directorate-General of Budget, Accounting, and Statistics, Executive Yuan.

———. 1977. *The report on 1976 industrial and commercial census, Taiwan-Fukien area, the Republic of China,* vol. 3. Taipei: Directorate-General of Budget, Accounting, and Statistics, Executive Yuan.

———. 1982. *The report on 1980 industrial and commercial census, Taiwan-Fukien area, the Republic of China,* vol. 3. Taipei: Directorate-General of Budget, Accounting, and Statistics, Executive Yuan.

———. 1988. *The report on 1986 industrial and commercial census, Taiwan-Fukien area, the Republic of China,* vol. 3. Taipei: Directorate-General of Budget, Accounting, and Statistics, Executive Yuan.

Directorate-General of Budget, Accounting, and Statistics (DGBAS), Executive Yuan, and Council for Economic Planning and Development (CEPD), Executive Yuan. 1987. *Report on the manpower utilization survey in Taiwan area, the Republic of China, 1986.* Taipei: Directorate-General of Budget, Acccounting, and Statistics, Executive Yuan, and Council for Economic Planning and Development, Executive Yuan.

————. 1988. *Report on the manpower utilization survey in Taiwan area, the Republic of China, 1987.* Taipei: Directorate-General of Budget, Accounting, and Statistics, Executive Yuan, and Council for Economic Planning and Development, Executive Yuan.

————. 1989. *Report on the manpower utilization survey in Taiwan area, the Republic of China, 1988.* Taipei: Directorate-General of Budget, Accounting, and Statitstics, Executive Yuan, and Council for Economic Planning and Development, Executive Yuan.

Dublin, Thomas. 1979. *Women at work: The transformation of work and community in Lowell, Massachusetts, 1826–1860.* New York: Columbia University Press.

Elson, D., and R. Pearson. 1984. The subordination of women and the internationalisation of factory production. In *Of marriage and the market: Women's subordination in international perspective,* ed. K. Young, C. Wolkowitz, and R. McCullagh, 18–40. London: CSE Books.

Fei, John C. H., Gustav Ranis, and Shirley W. Y. Kuo. 1979. *Growth with equity: The Taiwanese case.* New York: Oxford University Press.

Fernandez-Kelly, Maria Patricia, and Anna M. Garcia. 1989. Informalization at the core: Hispanic women, homework, and the advanced capitalist state. In *The informal economy: Studies in advanced and less developed countries,* ed. Alejandro Portes, Manuel Castells, and Lauren A. Benton, 247–64. Baltimore: John Hopkins University Press.

Freedman, Ronald, Baron Moots, Te-Hsiung Sun, and Mary Beth Weinberger. 1978. Household composition and extended kinship in Taiwan. *Population Studies* 32(1):65–80.

Freedman, Ronald, M. C. Chang, and T. H. Sun. 1982. Household composition, extended kinship, and reproduction in Taiwan, 1973–1980. *Population Studies* 36 (3):395–411.

Gallin, Bernard. 1966. *Hsin Hsing, Taiwan: A Chinese village in change.* Berkeley: University of California Press.

Gallin, Rita S. 1984a. *The impact of development on women's work and status: A case study from Taiwan.* East Lansing: Michigan State University, Women in International Development Publication Series, Working Paper 9.

————. 1984b. *Rural industrialization and Chinese women: A case study from Taiwan.* East Lansing: Michigan State University, Women in International Development Publication Series, Working Paper 47.

Gates, Hill. 1979. Dependency and the part-time proletariat in Taiwan. *Modern China* 5(3):381–408.

————. 1981. Ethnicity and social class. In *The anthropology of Taiwanese society,* ed. Emily Martin Ahern and Hill Gates, 241–81. Stanford, CA: Stanford University Press.

————. 1987. *Chinese working-class lives: Getting by in Taiwan.* Ithaca, NY: Cornell University Press.

————. 1989. The commoditization of Chinese women. *Signs: Journal of Women in Culture and Society* 14(4):799–832.

————. 1993. Cultural support for birth limitation among urban capital owning women. In *Chinese families in the post-Mao era*, ed. Debora Davis and Steven Harrell, 251–76. Berkeley: University of California Press.

Gereffi, Gary. 1989. Rethinking development theory: Insights from East Asia and Latin America. *Sociological Forum* 4(4):505–33.

Goldthorpe, John H. 1983. Women and class analysis: In defence of the conventional view. *Sociology* 17(4):465–88.

Greenhalgh, Susan. 1985. Sexual stratification: The other side of "growth with equity" in East Asia. *Population and Development Review* 11(2):265–314.

————. 1988. Families and networks in Taiwan's economic development. In *Contending approaches to the political economy of Taiwan*, ed. Edwin A. Winckler and Susan Greenhalgh, 224–45. Armonk, NY: M. E. Sharpe.

Griffen, Keith. 1973. An assessment of development in Taiwan. *World Development* 1:31–42.

Haggard, Stephan, and Tun-jen Cheng. 1987. State and foreign capital in the East Asian NIC. In *The political economy of the New Asian industrialism,* ed. Frederic C. Deyo, 84–135. Ithaca, NY: Cornell University.

Hamilton, Gary G, and Nicole W. Biggart. 1988. Market, culture, and authority: A comparative analysis of management and organization in the Far East. *American Journal of Sociology* 94(Supplement): S52–S94.

Harrell, Stevan. 1985. Why do the Chinese work so hard? Reflections on an entrepreneurial ethic. *Modern China* 11(2):203–26.

Hartmann, Heidi. 1979. The unhappy marriage of Marxism and feminism: Towards a more progressive union. *Capital and Class* 8:1–33.

Henderson, Jeffrey, and Richard P. Appelbaum. 1992. Situating the state in the East Asian development process. In *States and development in the Asian Pacific rim,* ed. Richard P. Appelbaum and Jeffrey Henderson, 1–26. Newbury Park, CA: Sage.

Ho, Samuel P. S. 1978. *Economic development of Taiwan, 1860–1970.* New Haven, CT: Yale University Press.

Hossfeld, Karen J. 1990. "Their logic against them": Contradictions in sex, race, and class in Silicon Valley. In *Women workers and global restructuring,* ed. Kathryn Ward, 149–78. Ithaca, NY: ILR Press, Cornell University.

Hsia, Ling-ching. 1990. Yige zizhu gonghui kangzheng lichens de anli diaocha baogao: jiegouxing chongtu yu geren xuexi (A study of the birth of an independent union: Social conflict and individual experience). *Taiwan Shehui Yaniiu Jikan* (Taiwan: A radical quarterly in social studies) 2(2):127–55.

Hsiung, Ping-Chun. 1990. The experiences of aboriginal prostitutes in Taiwan. Paper presented at the Annual Meeting of the National Women's Conference Committee, Manhattan Beach, CA, November 8–11, 1990.

————. (forthcoming). Between bosses and workers: The dilemma of a keen observer and a vocal feminist. In *Feminist dilemma in fieldwork,* ed. Diane L. Wolf. Boulder, CO: Westview Press.

Hsiung, Ray-Mei, Diana Wang, and Sue Ching Lu. 1989. Taiwan diqu kongchang nuzhuoyeyuan liangxing guanxi yu renkou jiaoyu zhi yenjiu (A study of the relationship between the sexes and population education among female factory workers in Taiwan). Proceedings of the Conference on Gender Roles and Changing Society, Women's Research Program, Institute of Sociology and Anthropology, National Tsing Hua University, April, pp. 173–98.

Hsu, Cheng-Kuang. 1976. Yanchun de shengtai yu jingii bianqian (Ecological change and economic activities in Yen village). *Minzusou Jikan* (Bulletin of the Institute of Ethnology, Academia Sinica) 42:1–39.

Hsu, Tsung-Kuo. 1989. Xingbei biaoqian de xueshu qongzhuo (Sex labeling of jobs in the academic profession). *Journal of Chinese Sociology* 13:129–68.

————. 1992. Nuren han nanren de gongzhuo yu jiating (Differences between women and men in their relations to work and family). Paper presented at the 87th Annual Meeting of the American Sociological Association, Pittsburgh, Pennsylvania.

Hu, Tai-Li. 1979. Xiaoshizhong de nongye shequ (The disappearing rural community). *Minzusou Jikan* (Bulletin of the Institute of Ethnology, Academia Sinica) 46:79–111.

————. 1982. *Xifu rumen* (When a daughter-in-law enters her husband's family). Taipei: Shibao Press.

————. 1984. *My mother-in-law's village: Rural industrialization and change in Taiwan*. Taipei: Institute of Ethnology, Academia Sinica. Monograph Series B, No. 13.

Huang, Fu-San. 1977. *Nukong yu Taiwan de kongyehua* (Female workers and Taiwan's industrialization). Taipei: Mutong Chubanshe.

Huang, Kuo-Long. 1984. Woguo zhuzhi zhong yuangong zhi gongzhuo manzu (Employees' work satisfaction in Taiwan). In *Zhongguo shi guanli (The Chinese style of management)*, ed. Gongshang Shibao Jingying Chongshu Xiaozu, 336–56. Taipei: Shibao Wenhua Chuban Shiye Youxian Kongsi.

Jinjibu Gongchang Jiaozheng Lianji Xiaozhu. 1988. *Gehang ye gongchang ming lu* (Factory directory for all industries). Taipei: Jinjibu Gongchang Jiaozheng Lianji Xiaozhu.

Johnson, Kay Ann. 1983. *Women, the family, and peasant revolution in China*. Chicago: University of Chicago Press.

Ka, Chih-Ming. 1993 *Taiwan dushi xiaoxing zhizhaoye de chuangye jingying yu shenchan zhuzhi* (Market, Social Networks, and the Production Organization of Small-Scale Industry in Taiwan). Taipei: Institute of Ethnology, Academia Sinica.

Kung, Lydia. 1976. Factory work and women in Taiwan: Changes in self-image and status. *Signs: Journal of Women in Culture and Society* 2(1):35–58.

————. 1983. *Factory women in Taiwan*. Ann Arbor, MI: UMI Research Press.

————. 1984. Taiwan garment workers. In *Lives: Chinese working women*, ed. Mary Sheridan and Janet W. Salaff, 109–22. Bloomington: Indiana University Press.

Kuo, Shirley, W. Y. 1983. *The Taiwan Economy in Transition*. Boulder, CO: Westview Press.

Lang, Olga. 1946. *Chinese family and society*. New Haven, CT: Yale University Press.

Laogong Xingzheng Zazhishe. 1989. *Laodong jizhunfa ji fusha faqui jieshiling* (Explantations of Labor Standard Law and related regulations). Taipei: Laogong Xingzheng Zazhishe.

————. 1990a. Laogon zhengche (Labor policy). In *Laozong jiaoyu chailiao* (Materials for workers' education). Taipei: Laogong Xingzheng Zazhishe.

————. 1990b. Laogon Lunli (The ethics between workers and capitalists). In *Laogong Jiaoyu chailiao* (Materials for workers' education). Taipei: Laogong Xingzheng Zazhishe.

————. 1990c. Laozi quanxi (Industrial relations). In *Laogong jiaoyu chailiao* (Materials for workers' education). Taipei: Laogong Xingzheng Zazhishe.

Lau, Lawrence J. 1990. The economy of Taiwan, 1981–88: A time of passages. In *Models of Development: A comparative study of economic growth in South Korea and Taiwan,* ed. Lawrence J. Lau, 183–216. San Francisco: ICS Press.

Li, May-Ji. 1987. Taiwan nuchuang yundong wangnali zou? (In which direction is Taiwan's feminist movement heading?). *Nuxing Zazhi* (Women's magazine), No. 246.

Li, Yeueh-Tuan, and Chih-Ming Ka. 1994. Xiaoxing qiye de jingying yu xingbie fengong: Yi Wufenpu chengyiye shequ wei anli de fenxi (Sexual division of labor and production organization in Wufenpu's small-scale industries). *Taiwan Shehui Yanjui Jikan* (Taiwan: A radical quarterly in social studies) 17: 41–81.

Lin, Alice P. 1988. *Grandmother had no name.* San Francisco: China Books and Peirodicals.

Liu, Paul K. C. 1984. Trends in female labor force participation in Taiwan: The transition toward higher technology activities. In *Women in the urban and industrial workforce, Southeast and East Asia,* ed. 75–99. Gavin Jones, Canberra: Australian National University.

Liu, Paul K. C., and Kuo-shu Hwang. 1987. *Relationships between changes in population, employment, and economic structure in Taiwan.* Taipei: Academia Sinica.

Liu, Yu-lan. 1985. *Taiwan diqu funu renli yunong huigu yu zhanwang* (Utilization of women's labor in Taiwan: Past and future). Taipei: Meizhi Tushu Gongsi.

Lu, Yu-Hsia. 1984. Women, work, and the family in a developing society: Taiwan. in *Women in the urban and industrial workforce, Southeast and East Asia,* ed. Gavin Jones, 339–66. Canberra: Australian National University.

Myer, Roger. 1990. Marketing the macho chew. *Free China Review* 40(5):46–55.

Mies, Maria, 1982. *The lace makers of Narsapur: Indian housewives produce for the world market.* London: Zed Press.

————. 1988. Capitalist development and subsistence production: Rural women in India. In *Women: The last colony,* ed. Maria Mies, Veronika Bennholdt-Thomsen, and Claudia von Werlhof, 27–45. London: Zed Books.

Myers, Ramon H. 1986. The economic development of the Republic of China on Taiwan, 1965–1981. In *Models of development: A comparative study of economic growth in South Korea and Taiwan,* ed. Lawrence J. Lau, 13–64. San Francisco: Institute for Contemporary Studies.

Niehoff, Justin D. 1987. The villager as industrialist: Ideologies of household manufacturing in rural Taiwan. *Modern China* 13(3):278–309.

Ong, Aihwa. 1987. *Spirits of resistance and capitalist discipline: Factory women in Malaysia.* Albany: State University of New York.

Orru, Marco. 1991. The institutional logic of small-firm economies in Italy and Taiwan. *Studies in Compartive International Development* 26(1):3–28.

Oxfeld, Ellen. 1993. *Blood, sweat, and mahjong.* Ithaca, NY: Cornell University.

Patai, Daphne, 1991. U.S. academics and Third World women: Is ethical research possible? In *Women's words: The feminist practice of oral history,* ed. Sherna Berger Gluck and Daphne Patai, 137–53. New York: Routledge.

Piore, Michael J., and Charles F. Sabel. 1984. *The second industrial divide: Possibilities of prosperity.* New York: Basic Books.

Portes, Alejandro, Manuel Castells, and Lauren A. Benton. 1989. *The informal economy: studies in advanced and less developed countries.* Baltimore: John Hopkins University Press.

Portes, Alejandro, and Saskia Sassen-Koob. 1987. Making it underground: Comparative material on the urban informal sector in Western market economies. *American Journal of Sociology* 93:30–61.

Ranis, Gustav. 1979. Industrial Development. In *Economic growth and structural change in Taiwan: The postwar experience of the Republic of China,* ed. Walter Galenson, 206–62. Ithaca, NY: Cornell University Press.

Rubin, Lillian B. 1976. *Worlds of pain: Life in the working-class family.* New York: Basic Books.

San, Gee. 1988. Ruhe liding woguo jiben gongzhi (How to stipulate minimum wage levels in Taiwan, R.O.C.). *Renwen yu Shehui Kexue Jikan* (Journal of social sciences and philosophy) 1(1):15–40.

Sassen-Koob, Saskia. 1989. New York City's informal economy. In *The informal economy: Studies in advanced and less developed countries,* ed. Alejandro Portes, Manuel Castells, and Lauren A. Benton, 60–77. Baltimore: John Hopkins University Press.

Scitovsky, Tibor. 1986. Economic development in Taiwan and South Korea, 1965–1981. In *Models of development: A comparative study of economic growth in South Korea and Taiwan,* ed. Lawrence J. Lau, 135–95. San Francisco: Institute for Contemporary Studies.

Scott, James C. 1985. *Weapons of the weak: Everyday forms of peasant resistance.* New Haven, CT: Yale University Press.

———. 1990. *Domination and the arts of resistance: Hidden transcripts.* New Haven, CT: Yale University Press.

Shi, Jiqing. 1987. Zhiye funu de zhangai saipao (Obstacles for female professionals). *Funu Xinzhi* (Awaking) 59:8–12.

Shieh, Gwo-Shyong. 1990. Manufacturing "bosses": Subcontracting networks under dependent capitalism in Taiwan. Ph.D. dissertation, department of sociology, University of California, Berkeley.

*Shijie Ribao,* September 8, 1990.

Sili Shijian Jianzheng Jingji Zhuanke Xuexiao. 1985. *Mama jiaoshi buchong jiaocai* (Supplementary instructional materials for Mothers' Workshops). Taizhong: Taiwan Shengzhengfu.

Skoggard, Ian A. 1993. Dependency and rural industrialization in Taiwan: The history and organization of Taiwan's shoe industry. PH.D. dissertation, department of anthropology, City University of New York.

Stacey, Judith. 1983. *Patriarchy and socialist revolution in China.* Berkeley: University of California Press.

————. 1991. Can there be a feminist ethnography? In *Women's words: The feminist practice of oral history,* ed. Sherna Berger Gluck and Daphne Patai, 111–20. New York: Routledge.

Standing, Guy. 1989. Global feminisation through flexible labor. World Employment Programme Research, Working Paper 31. Geneva: ILO.

Stepick, Alex. 1989. Miami's two informal sectors. In *The informal economy: Studies in advanced and less developed countries,* ed. Alejandro Portes, Manuel Castells, and Lauren A. Benton, 111–34. Baltimore: John Hopkins University Press.

Stites, Richard. 1982. Small-scale industry in Yingge, Taiwan. *Modern China* 8(2): 247–79.

————. 1985. Industrial work as an entrepreneurial strategy. *Modern China* 11(2): 227–46.

Taiwan Shengzhengfu Gongbao. 1990. *Executive Yuan, Document No. 17050, June 26, 1989.* Taizhong: Taiwan Shengzhengfu.

Taiwan Shengzhengfu Shehuichu. 1977. *Mama duben* (Mothers' readers), 10 vols. Taizhong: Taiwan Shengzhenfu Shehuichu.

Taiwansheng Mamajiaoshi Fudao Renyuan Yanxihui. 1987. *Taiwansheng 74, 75 Niandu Shequ Mamajiaoshi Fudao Renyuan Zuotanhui Zonghe Jishi* (Proceedings of the 1985–86 Community Mothers' Workshop Supervisors' Seminar). Taizhong: Taiwansheng Mamajiaoshi Fudao Renyuan Yanxihui.

Taiwanshenzhengfu Shehuichu n d *Shequ fazhan zhi lilun yu shishi* (Theory and practice of community development). Taizhong: Taiwanshenzhengfu Shehuichu.

Taiwan Shengzhengfu Yanjiu Kaohe Fazhan Weiyuanhui. 1983. *Taiwansheng shinianlai shequ fazhan chengxiao zhi pinejian ji weilai fanzhan zhi yanjiu* (Evaluation of the ten-year Community Development Program in Taiwan and its future direction). Taipei: Taiwanshengzhengfu Yanjiu Kaohe Fazhan Weiyuanhui.

Thorbecke, Erik. 1979. Agricultural development. In *Economic growth and structural change in Taiwan: The postwar experience of the Republic of China,* ed. Walter Galenson, 132–205. Ithaca, NY: Cornell University Press.

*The Economist.* 1993. A survey of Italy: Until the fat lady sings. 1327(7817):1–22.

*Time.* 1992. Taiwan, all alone and feeling blue? 140(10):51.

Tsay, Ching-lung. 1985. Zhanhou Taiwan jiaoyu yu laodongli fazhan zhi xingbie chayi (Sex differentials in educational attainment and labor force development in

Taiwan). In *Funu zai Guojia Fazhan Guochengzhong de Jiaose Yantaohui Lunwenji* (Proceedings of Conference on the Role of Women in the National Development Process in Taiwan), ed. Population Studies Center, 277–308. Taipei: National Taiwan University, Population Studies Center.

Tsung, Shiu-Kuen Fan. 1978. Moms, nuns, and hookers: Extrafamilial alternatives for village women in Taiwan. Ph.D. dissertation, department of anthropology, University of California, San Diego.

U.S. Bureau of the Census. *Statistical abstract of the United States*, various years. Washington, DC.

Wallerstein, Immanuel, 1974. *The modern world-system 1: Capitalist agriculture and the origins of the world economy*. New York: Academic.

Ward, Kathryn, 1986. *Women and transnational corporation employment: A world-system and feminist analysis*. East Lansing: Michigan State University, Women in International Development Publication Series, Working Paper 120.

Weiwei Furen. 1987. Xuanze senghuo fangshe de jihui (The wisdom of choosing a lifestyle). In *Yige nuren de changzhan* (A woman's growing up), 16–17. Taipei, Yuanliu Chubanshe.

Werlhof, Claudia von. 1988. The proletarian is dead: Long live the housewife! In *Women: The last colony,* ed. Maria Mies, Veronika Bennholdt-Thomsen, and Claudia von Werlhof, 168–81. London: Zed Books.

Wolf, Margery. 1972. *Women and the family in rural Taiwan*. Stanford, CA: Stanford University Press.

Wong, Siu-lun. 1985. The Chinese family firm: A model. *The British Journal of Sociology* 36(1):58–72.

Wu, Guang-he. n.d. *Laogong fagui* (The union law). Taichung: Kuaiji Chuban She.

Wu, Hui-lin, and Teir-chen Chow. 1992. *Zhongxiao qiye de kunjing yu yinying* (Obstacles and coping strategies of small and medium size enterprises). Taipei: Chunghua Institution for Economic Research.

Xie, Dong-min. 1989. Weishenmo yao Chuangban Mamajiaoshi? (Why do we establish Mothers' Workshops?). In *Taiwansheng Mamajiaoshi Fudao Regyuan Yanxihui Shouche* (Handbook for supervisors of the Mothers' Workshops). Taizhong: Taiwansheng Mamajiaoshi Fudao Renyuan Yanxihui.

Xie, Meng-xiong. 1985. Shequ Mamajiaoshi yu jiazheng jiaoyu (The community Mothers' Workshop and homemaking education). *Shequ Fazhan Jikan* (Community development quarterly) 29:60–61.

Xinzhengyuan Jingji Jianshe Weiyuanhui. 1978. *Ruhe yi shequ fazhan fangshi tuixing jiating faye zhi yanjiu* (How to promote family subsidiary work through the Community Development Program). Taipei: Xinzhengyuan Jingji Jianshe Weiyuanhui.

Yang Ch'ing-Ch'u. 1976. Guipabi yu suibengsan (Wage workers and capitalist owners). *Lianhe Bao,* June.

———. 1977. Gongchang wuhui (Dance party in the factory). In *Yang Ch'ing-Ch'u xiaoshuoxuan* (Selected stories of Yang Ch'ing-Ch'u), 134–49. Taipei: Lanjing.

Yao, Esther Lee. 1981. Successful professional Chinese women in Taiwan. *Cornell Journal of Social Relations* 16(1):39–55.

Yen, Han-wen Edwin. 1989. Jinshinianlai Taiwan diqu xinjiaoyu yanjiu zhi huigu (A review of sex education in Taiwan over the last ten years). Proceedings of the Conference on Gender Roles and Changing Society, Women's Research Program, Institute of Sociology and Anthropology, National Tsing Hua University, April, pp. 287–304.

Zhao, Shoubo. 1984. Taiwansheng tuixing Mamajiaoshi zhi xianzai yu weilai (The current status and future prospects of Mothers' Workshops in Taiwan). *Shequ Fazhan Jikan* (Community development quarterly) 28:24–27.

Zheng, Wei-Yuan, and Liao Rong-Li. 1985. *Ruibianzhong de Taiwan funu* (Taiwanese women in a changing world). Taipei: Dayang Chubanshe.

*Zhongguo Lutan.* 1982. Dangqin shehuizhong funu wenti zhi tantao zhuotanhui (A workshop on women's issues on current society). *Zhongguo Luntan* (Chinese tribune of opinions) 13(11):11–21.

———. 1989. *Nuxing zhishi fenzi yu Taiwan Fazhan* (The female intellectual and Taiwan's development). Taipei: Zhongguo Luntan Zhazishe.

Ziping, 1982. Beige heshi liao? (Where is the end to all these sad songs?). *Funu Xingzi* (Awaking) 4:12–17.

# Index